Language, Learning and Education

Language, Learning and Education

Selected papers from the Bristol Study:
'Language at Home and at School'

Gordon Wells

NFER-NELSON

Ministry of Education, Ontario
Information Centre, 13th Floor,
Mowat Block, Queen's Park,
Toronto, Ont. M7A 1L2

Published by The NFER-NELSON Publishing Company Ltd.,
Darville House, 2 Oxford Road East,
Windsor, Berkshire SL4 1DF

and in the United States of America by

NFER-NELSON, 242 Cherry Street, Philadelphia,
PA 19106 – 1906.
Tel: (215) 238 0939. Telex: 244489.

First Published 1985
©1985, Gordon Wells

Library of Congress Cataloging in Publication data

Wells, C. Gordon.
    Language, learning, and education.

1. Language acquisition – Addresses, essays, lectures.
2. Children – Language – Addresses, essays, lectures.
3. Language and education – Addresses, essays, lectures.
I. Language at home and at school. II.   Title.
P118.W418   1985   401'.9   85-21557
ISBN 0–7005–1031–1

All rights reserved, including translation. No part of this
publication may be reproduced or transmitted in any form or by
any means, electronic or mechanical, including photocopying,
recording or duplication in any information storage and retrieval
system, without permission in writing from the publishers.

Photoset by David John (Services) Ltd, Maidenhead.

Printed in Great Britain by A. Wheaton & Co. Ltd., Exeter

ISBN 0 7005 1047 8
Code 8242 02 1

Contents

Foreword vii

Preface to the second edition xiii

Chapter 1	Talking and Learning	1
Chapter 2	A Naturalistic Approach to the Study of Language Development	26
Chapter 3	Enabling Factors in Adult–Child Discourse	43
Chapter 4	Language and Learning: an Interactional Perspective	58
Chapter 5	Some Antecedents of Early Educational Attainment	74
Chapter 6	Talking with Children: the Complementary Roles of Parents and Teachers	100
Chapter 7	Story Reading and the Development of Symbolic Skills	132
Chapter 8	The Relevance of Applied Linguistics for Teachers of Reading	141
Chapter 9	Language, Learning and the Curriculum	152

Appendix 1 176

Appendix 2 180

References 183

Foreword

In 1972, when the Bristol Language Development Research Programme began, I had no idea that, ten years later, we should still be recording some of the same children. The research began as a study of pre-school language and our primary aim was to chart the sequence of development and to investigate possible causes of differences between children in the rate at which development proceeds. But, from the beginning, there was also an educational concern. Is early language experience as important for success in school as the arguments about 'linguistic disadvantage' suggest? If so, what sort of linguistic experience is characteristic of those who succeed in school and how can schools help those who are initially less successful?

Follow-up studies of two smaller groups from the original sample have given us an opportunity to investigate these questions in considerable detail, and eventually we shall be able to look back from the vantage point of the last year of primary schooling to evaluate the relative contributions of home and school to the level of attainment reached at that stage.

In the meantime, the completion of ten years of research seems to call for at least an interim gathering together of the main strands of the investigation, as they bear on the educational questions outlined above. It is with that aim that the papers that follow have been collected in one volume. Written at different times and with different audiences in mind, they are inevitably somewhat repetitive. They also differ in style of presentation. from the relatively informal overview of the main findings, with discussion of their implications, to the detailed and technical presentation of the results of one particular phase of the programme.

At the same time there is, I hope, some continuity and coherence as the same questions are reconsidered from different perspectives and the longitudinal data from the same group of children analysed in different ways.

Nevertheless, this remains a collection of independent papers and should be treated as such. Few readers will wish to read all of them and probably none will wish to read from cover to cover. The following paragraphs, therefore, provide a brief indication of the contents of the various chapters and allow me to acknowledge my debts to my co-authors, where appropriate, and to the journals in which the articles originally appeared.

Plan of the Book

Chapter 1, *Talking and Learning*, is intended as an introduction to the rest of the volume. It is in fact a transcription – slightly edited to render it more readable – of a lecture given at the Annual General Meeting of the Child Development Society at the University of London Institute of Education in October 1980 and subsequently published in the Society's *Newsletter* (Vol. 30, 1981). In the first part of the lecture I described the main phases of the research and then went on to mention some of the major findings. Quite a large part of the lecture was devoted to playing examples of conversation recorded in homes and schools, and so none of the topics raised is developed in great detail. Nevertheless, I think the paper gives a fairly balanced overview of the research programme as a whole.

Chapter 2, *A Naturalistic Approach to the Study of Language Development*, provides a more technical account of the methods of observation and analysis used in the study. Although probably not of interest to many readers, such an account provides essential information for those who wish to assess the reliability and representativeness of the results reported in the other chapters. A second reason for including this paper is that the discussion it contains of the difficulties associated with the 'naturalistic approach' – and of the methods adopted in the attempt to resolve them – may be of benefit to others who are considering carrying out a similar type of research. Even with the benefit of hindsight, I would still advocate the collection of spontaneous conversational data, but I would now almost certainly wish to complement such recordings with samples of more systematically elicited speech.

This paper was presented at a symposium on Spoken and Written Language that I was asked to organize for the British Educational Research Association Annual Conference in London in September 1976. Although a summary was published in *Research Intelligence*, the paper has never before been published in its entirety.

As we began to obtain results from the analyses described in Chap. 2, it became apparent that there were substantial differences between children in their rate of language development. This was not unexpected. However, what was less expected, given the prevailing views on 'linguistic disadvantage', was the generally rather low level of correlation that we found between rate of language development and class of family background. This, together with the low correlations obtained between scores from tests and measures derived from spontaneous speech, led me to express grave reservations about any simple statements of relationship between pre-school oral language development, class and subsequent attainment (see Chap. 5).

More important than class of family background in accounting for variation in language development, we believe, is the quality of the child's conversational experience. Chapter 3, *Enabling Factors in Adult–Child Discourse*, reports a study carried out by Rod Ellis to explore this possibility. By comparing the speech addressed to three groups of children – early fast developers, late fast developers and slow developers – he was able to show that there were significant differences between the three groups in the frequencies with which different types of utterance were addressed to them and in the contexts in which most conversation occurred. The study was initially presented as a dissertation for the degree of M.Ed. in the Language and Learning Programme and a revised version was subsequently published as a joint paper by Ellis and myself in *First Language* (Vol. 1, pp.46–62, 1980).

By the time the second edition of this collection came to be prepared, the first phase of the research had been completed and the final report was about to be published (Wells, 1985a). Chapter 4, *Language and Learning: an Interactional Perspective*, reviews some of the main findings from that report and offers an interpretation of them. The key to the enigma of where language comes from, I suggest, is to be found in interaction: interaction between learners who are predisposed to make sense of their experience, including their experience of linguistic communication, and a community of more mature language users who provide the evidence on which the learners construct their representation of the language system. Differences in rate of learning can be explained, at least in part, in terms of the quality of this evidence and of the manner in which it is provided. In this second sense also, therefore, interaction provides the key. In the form of conversation, linguistic interaction is both the means and the goal for language learning. This chapter was written as a contribution to a special edition of *Educational Analysis* (Wells and Nicholls, 1985 and I am grateful to Falmer Press for permission to reprint it.

Chapter 5, *Some Antecedents of Early Educational Attainment*,

x *Language, Learning and Education*

takes the longitudinal study one stage further and reports the results of a statistical analysis of the data from the second follow-up study, 'Language in the Transition from Home to School'. The really striking finding from this study was the overwhelming importance of what we called 'Knowledge of Literacy' as a predictor of educational attainment at age seven. By comparison, differences in oral language ability were of much less significance. This finding is compared with Bernstein's theory of the relationship between class, code and educational attainment and certain similarities and differences noted. This paper was originally published in the *British Journal of Sociology of Education* (Vol. 2, pp.181-200, 1981).

Although home and school are often set in opposition to each other by educationalists who seek for a linguistic explanation for differences in educational achievement, it is important that, from the child's point of view, they should be complementary. Chapter 6, *Talking with Children: the Complementary Roles of Parents and Teachers*, compares samples of adult–child conversation recorded in the two settings of home and school in order to see how far this is indeed the case. On the whole, by comparison with parents, teachers are seen to be restricted in the style of interaction that they typically adopt, with the 'display' question sequence being the predominant mode, whatever the task in which the child is engaged. Against this background, I suggest that a more varied style of interaction in the classroom would have two advantages, first in easing the transition from home to school and, secondly, in allowing the type of talk to be more appropriately matched to the different sorts of learning that teachers are trying to promote. This paper was first presented to the Early Years Commission at the Annual Conference of the National Association for the Teaching of English in 1977 and subsequently published in *English in Education* (Vol. 12, 2, pp.15-38, 1978).

In Chapter 7, *Story Reading and the Development of Symbolic Skills*, written in 1982 for the *Australian Journal of Reading*, I return to the theme of the importance of early experience of literacy and argue, with support from the Bristol data, that it is the experience of listening to stories, rather than mere familiarity with the visual representation of meaning, that provides such a beneficial preparation for the language demands of the classroom. Because written language creates its own context of meaning, it requires the reader (or listener in the case of a story read aloud) to pay attention to the verbal message alone and so draws the child's attention to the power that language has to create 'possible worlds' through words. The combination of stories and non-directive exploratory conversation about them provides, I suggest, one of the most enriching forms of language experience for children at any age.

The last two chapters focus more directly on the role of the teacher, and make a plea for a greater emphasis on self-directed learning. Chapter 8, *The Relevance of Applied Linguistics for Teachers of Reading*, was written with Bridie Raban, the co-director of the follow-up study entitled 'Children Learning to Read'. Commissioned for a volume entitled *Applied Linguistics and Reading*, edited by R. Schafer, for the International Reading Association (IRA, 1979), this paper argues that teachers should be much more cautious about accepting the theories of linguists and psychologists as a basis for classroom practice in the teaching of reading and writing. Research on lanugage can provide helpful insights about the nature of language but, in the last resort, the theories that will be most helpful for teachers are those that they construct for themselves.

The final chapter, *Language, Learning and the Curriculum*, is an attempt to pull together the various themes addressed in the earlier papers. It was written in 1982 to appear in *Education 3–13*. Focusing on the communicative context of learning, I argue that, just as successful conversation is collaborative and negotiatory, so the most effective learning will occur when responsibility for the choice and presentation of learning tasks is shared with the teacher and with other learners. Both teachers and taught, I suggest, will find life in school more challenging and rewarding when learning is seen as a collaborative activity in which all participants are recognized to be actively and responsibly engaged in the making of meaning.

In presenting this collection of papers, I should like to acknowledge the support received from the various agencies who have funded the research: the Boots Charitable Trust, the Nuffield Foundation, the Social Science Research Council and the Spencer Foundation. I should also particularly like to thank the children and their parents and teachers for allowing us to observe them and to quote from those observations. Finally, I should like to thank the many members of the research team who have carried out the laborious tasks of collecting, transcribing, coding and analysing the data. To the following I owe a particular debt of gratitude: Jan Adams, Chris Amos, Sally Barnes, Allayne Bridges, Sally Davis, Rod Ellis, Jo Evans, Linda Ferrier, Peter French, Mary Gutfreund, John Homewood, Margaret MacLure, Frank Maddix, Martin Montgomery, Cliff Moon, Tricia Nash, Dorinda Offord, Bridie Raban, David Satterly, Chris Sinha, Valerie Walkerdine and Bencie Woll. As colleagues and students working within the

xii *Language, Learning and Education*

research programme they have played a major part in the development of the ideas presented in the chapters that follow. I am most grateful for their help.

Gordon Wells
Centre for the Study of Language and Communication
University of Bristol
June 1982

Preface to the second edition

In revising this collection of papers for the publication of a second edition, I have taken the opportunity to make some changes in order to reduce the amount of repetition and to bring it up-to-date. In particular, I have omitted two of the original chapters and substituted another which was written more recently.

The first edition was produced to mark the end of the first decade of the Bristol study, 'Language at Home and at School'. By chance, the need for a second edition coincides with my leaving Bristol. I should like to take this opportunity, therefore, to thank all those who have contributed to the achievements of the study up to this point and to wish success to those who continue it in the future.

Gordon Wells
Ontario Institute for Studies in Education
Toronto
September 1984

CHAPTER 1
Talking and Learning

The topic I have chosen – 'Talking and Learning' – is a way of pulling together the various strands of the longitudinal research project that we have been engaged in for the last ten years. However, the project is still far from being completed, so any results that I can give must be treated as interim results which may need to be modified as the work progresses. What I propose here is to spend some time describing the first phase of the research, that is the study of language development in the pre-school years, then to go on to describe the follow-up study of some of the children in their infant school classrooms and, finally, to consider some of the implications that I think this study has for those of us who are concerned with the education of young children.

The juxtaposition of 'Talking' and 'Learning' is intended to emphasize the close connection that exists between these two activities. Certainly, in early childhood, it is through talking that children learn, and what they learn is both their native language and the experience that is expressed through that language. In fact the two things go on simultaneously and the most important feature of a child's language experience is that it is conversational in nature.

Our research has not yet had time to focus on talk between children and their peers. I am not sure how important such talk is, although it clearly forms a considerable part of some children's language experience. But when we think that not all children of pre-school age have siblings and yet they still learn to talk, it seems pretty clear that it is the adults who are the more important conversational partners.

So, talking with adults can be seen as providing the context in which children learn the language of their culture, and simultaneously learn the way in which experience is organized within that culture. When children go to school they find that language provides the medium of instruction and, as they will discover somewhat later, it is also the chief medium through which their learning is assessed. For all these reasons, therefore, I think one can argue that the study of language development justifies serious attention from anybody working in the field of education and so I do not feel I need to provide any further justification for the amount of time and energy that has been devoted to our longitudinal research programme.

The first phase of the research, which began in 1972, was a study of 128 children all born, or at least residing, in Bristol at the beginning of the study. Half of the children were aged 15 months at that time and half were aged 39 months. The aim was to follow each child for 2¼ years, making regular observations at three-monthly intervals, so that we could: (1) chart the course of language development for a representative sample of children and (2) try to identify some of the major environmental factors that influence the course of development.

By 1975, we were getting to the end of the recording of those children and at that time Bridie Raban, who had done a great deal of work in the field of reading, suggested that it would be an ideal opportunity to study the connection between pre-school experience and the early stages of learning to read. So the second stage of the study, 'Children Learning to Read' was carried out between 1975 and 1977 under her joint direction. During this time we followed 20 of the older group of children, observing them in their classrooms once a month and keeping a continuous written record of their activities for a complete morning; focusing, obviously, on activities connected with reading and writing.

One of the main conclusions from that study was that any difference between schools that affects the progress children make in learning to read was not to be found in the different amounts of time that children spent on different activities connected with reading and writing. It did not seem to make much difference how that time was distributed. However, we did feel that there were qualitative differences between the teachers in the way they introduced the children to reading and organized and commented on the children's activities and that these had a significant effect on children's progress. But, because we only kept a pencil and paper record, we were not able to measure these essential qualitative differences between teachers. In fact it became clear that, in order to study the influence of teachers, we would need to make verbatim recordings of the interactions in which they engaged with children. So we planned a third phase for the research in which we would do just that.

The third phase started in 1977, when we began a follow-up study involving 32 children from the younger age group, children who had first been observed in their homes at the age of 15 months. We recorded them again in their homes before they started school and we interviewed their parents to find out about the home environment and about any ways in which they had prepared the children for school. Then we made a number of observations of the children in their classrooms, using audio and video recording equipment. We tested the children at the age of five, on entry to school, and again just before their seventh birthday, and we asked the teachers to make an assessment of the children at the same ages. Finally we interviewed the parents again when each child was aged seven to find out in what ways they had been assisting the child with his or her work at school. We have just completed the first round of analysis of that project and I shall report some of the findings later.

Simultaneously with that phase we made a return to the pre-school recordings of these 32 children in an attempt to understand more clearly the nature of conversation and the role that conversation plays in the acquisition of a first language. This has been a rather more theoretical research project because, although a certain amount of work had been done on the description of conversation, no totally satisfactory descriptive model was available in 1977, so most of our time has been spent in developing a way of describing conversation that would begin to explain the development that is so evident when one listens to the recordings we have made.

Work on that phase is currently at a standstill, as the various members of the research team have moved on to other institutions. However, we shall be picking up the threads again in the not-too-distant future.

At the present time we are engaged in the construction of a scale of language development. If one has made observations of a large number of children and found, as we have, that there is a common pattern of development, then one can use the information obtained longitudinally (that is, over time) to show which aspects of language develop before which others. We are now converting this into a developmental scale, which we believe will have two kinds of use. First, as a way of assessing a child's level of development at any age and of giving an indication of what he or she is likely to learn next, so that if one wishes to intervene in any way, one knows what to concentrate on at that particular point in the child's development. Secondly, as an instrument for researchers who need to compare the developmental level of children at any particular age. This project has only been running for one year so far and still has a long way to go before we produce instruments suitable for use by other people.

I hope that this brief overview has given a general idea of the scope of our research. It may also have given some idea of the magnitude of the total undertaking which, had I been able to see its size in a crystal ball before I started, I do not think I would ever have embarked upon!

However, given that we have collected and analysed this wide range of information about a representative sample of children, their language development and their early learning in school, I am in a position to report a number of findings which I hope will be of general interest.

Similarities and Differences in Development

The first and perhaps the most important single finding from our study is that, with one exception, all the children that we have observed had achieved a mastery of English by the time they started school. That is to say, they had a basic command of the grammar of English and a vocabulary of several thousand words, and were using these resources to communicate effectively with their family and neighbours on a wide variety of topics and for a wide variety of purposes.

Secondly, as I have already suggested, the general picture that emerges is a common pattern of development across the children: the same order of learning of the various systems of language. But whilst we found a similar sequence of development, we also found very considerable variation in rate of development. Just as an indication of that variation, I shall quote one figure.

If one takes a very rough measure of language development, such as mean length of utterance, one can say that the most advanced children at the age of 3½ had a mean length of utterance which was not attained by the average child until the age of five, and the least advanced children at 3½ still only had a mean length of utterance which was attained by the average child at about the age of 2¼ years. So there was a difference of nearly three years in this sample of 128 children at the age of 3½. Now that is a very considerable range of development and one which makes the first claim all the more surprising: that all the children had achieved a basic mastery of English by the time they started school. But it also gives some idea of how far ahead the most advanced were by the age of five, and therefore of the problems that face teachers in the infant school reception class.

Naturally we have also attempted to discover some of the possible reasons for this large variation in rate of development. We started with a consideration of sex difference, as there is a very common belief that girls make more rapid progress than boys in language development. Well, we have not found that to be the case, although on one or two measures the girls were slightly in advance, in particular they tended to be more talkative than the boys. But on some measures the boys were ahead of the girls. Overall it is not possible to say that either sex was more advanced than the other.

We have also looked at what we have called 'Class of Family Background', because again there is a generally held belief that lower-class children tend to be retarded compared to their middle-class peers. Here, too, we have found very little evidence of a class-of-family-background difference in the pre-school years. It is true that the most advanced children tend to come from the upper end of the family background scale and the least advanced children from the lower end of the scale. But, overall, the vast majority of children show no association between rate of development and class of family background. This makes it all the more disturbing that, as soon as we observed the children in school, we found the anticipated strong relationship between family background and educational attainment (see Chap. 5). This is an issue to which I shall return later.

However, the broad demographic differences such as those of sex or family background are not really the best place to look, it seems to me, if one wants to explain variation in rate of development. If children learn to talk through conversing with others, it is surely there that one ought to look: at the quality of their conversational experience. And indeed that is precisely what we have been attempting to do.

Conversation at Home

It is already well known that adults typically modify their speech when talking to young children. Parents and most other adults – in fact even fairly young children – produce short, grammatically complete and well-formed utterances when talking to a two-year-old. They tend to use an exaggerated pitch range and a lot of rising intonation, in order, it appears, to attract and hold the child's attention – as it were to point out the fact that it is the child who is being addressed, and also to focus his or her attention. These are universal characteristics of adults' speech to young children, found not only in studies of English but of almost every language throughout the world (see Snow and Ferguson, 1977). If that is the case, though, such broad adjustments by adults cannot really explain the difference between children in language development, since they are part of all children's experience. So one needs to look more closely at the quality of the speech addressed to these young children to see if there are important differences between parents in this respect.

At the age of two, we have been able to identify a number of features of parental speech that seem to be associated with the children's rate of development. One of these is the frequency of direct requests when controlling the child, either for his or her own safety or for the general well-being of child and parent. There are a great many short, imperative utterances to the fast-developing children. A second characteristic of speech addressed at this age to the fast-developing children is a very high proportion of utterances which pick up and extend the topic of the child's previous utterance or ongoing activity. It is as if the adult produces language which is ideally matched to the child's current focus of attention or rather to the *shared* focus of attention, expressing an interest in what he or she is doing or communicating, and helping them to extend their understanding of this shared topic.

Thirdly, we found that, at this specific age, a high proportion of questions that require a yes/no answer is important to the child. Now, that might appear to be contrary to what one would expect, because such utterances by an adult make rather small demands upon the child as a respondent. However, it seems that the importance of such questions may be rather that they point up certain features of the grammatical structure of the language. Also, perhaps, because they make such small demands on children, they are easier for them to process at this stage of development.

Another important feature of the speech addressed to the fast-developing children at this age is the sheer amount of adult talk. Now that is, I suppose, something that one could have anticipated but, because there has not been a study before ours that has taken a large, representative sample of children and recorded them in such a way that an identical amount of time is sampled in each recording, it has not previously been possible to compare the amount of speech addressed to different children. Here too we have found extreme variation. For example, amongst the children that we have been focusing on most recently, when they are just into the two-word utterance stage, we found that, in a recording which consisted of eighteen 90-second samples, the child who received the least speech had 36 utterances addressed to her, whereas the child who received the most speech in exactly the same amount of time had more than 300 utterances addressed to him. Now that is an enormous range. Not surprisingly, the children who received the most language tended by and large to make the most rapid progress. But it is not straightforward, because some of the rapid developers were not amongst the children who received the largest amount of speech. Some of those who were 'bathed in language', as the expression is, did not make particularly rapid development. So it is not quantity alone that is important. But obviously, if the quality is high and there is a lot of it, then the child is well set to make rapid progress.

In summary, if I tried to characterize the ideal sort of conversational experience for a two-year-old, I think I should say something like this. The contributions that adults make to the shared conversation should express an attitude of reciprocity. They should treat the child as an equal conversational partner, who has something interesting to say, and they should support the child's attempts to communicate and extend his or her contributions. By contrast, an adult style of conversation which is dominating and didactic is not helpful to a child of this age. I can illustrate what I mean by quoting examples from two different children at exactly the same age.

But first of all I shall set out a short extract from a slightly earlier stage. Conventions of the transcription are as follows: the child's speech is on the left, the adult's or anyone else's speech is in the centre and information about the context is on the right. The symbol (v) means that the name was used vocatively to call for attention. (Full details of conventions can be found in Appendix 1.)

Mark is in the kitchen with his mother. He is looking into a mirror.

Mark: Mummy(v)
      Mummy   [Mk sees reflection of
                      M: What?   mother]
Mark: There. there   [Mk sees himself]
      Mark
                      M: Is that Mark?
Mark: Mummy
                      M: Mm (confirming)
Mark: Mummy
                      M: Yes that's Mummy
Mark: Mummy (acknowl.)
      Mummy(v)
                      M: Mm
Mark: There Mummy
      Mummy(v)
      There. Mark there

8   Language, Learning and Education

              M: Look at Helen   [Helen is his sister]
                   She's going to
                   sleep

            (long pause)

Mark: /εəæ/(=look at that)   [Mk can see birds in
      Birds Mummy(v)   the garden]
              M: Mm (acknowl.)
Mark: Jubs (=birds)
              M: What are they
                   doing?
Mark: Jubs bread
              M: Oh look!
                   They're eating the berries
                   aren't they?
Mark: Yeh
              M: That's their food
                   They have berries for dinner
Mark: Oh (acknowl.)

    The characteristics that I have already mentioned are very clear in that short extract. First, it is noticeable that the child has very limited resources. Yet one gets a very strong feeling from that short extract that there is a real conversation going on, even though it is the mother who is doing most of the work. It is like when children are learning to catch a ball. What one has to do is to throw it so that it lands firmly in their cupped arms; then one has to be prepared to rush around to catch it wherever they throw it. That is precisely what the mother is doing here. She is aiming the conversational ball so it lands easily in the child's rather clumsy hands and then fielding the return from whatever direction the ball goes in when he throws it.
    Secondly, in these utterances the mother uses rising tone: *Is that Mark.... Mm.... Yes, that's Mummy.* All the time saying, in effect, 'I am really fascinated by what you're telling me, do go on, I am listening and very interested to hear more.' This what you might call the 'Sustaining Strategy'.
    The third point that one notices is that out of the three short sequences of conversation – one about what Mark can see in the mirror, the second about Helen going to sleep, and the third about the birds having their dinner – the two that actually get anywhere are the ones that are introduced by Mark. Where the mother tries to introduce a topic into the conversation, it does not get off the

ground. I think that is very significant. Children at this age are egocentric. That is to say it is only when they initiate the topic that they are able to play a full part in its discussion. It is very much more difficult for them to take the point of view of another person introducing a topic that is not of their own choosing.

Finally I should like to draw attention to the last sequence of conversation about the birds and their dinner. In effect, what happens is that Mark introduces the topic: birds. Mother says: 'What are they doing?' She invites him to expand on the topic that he has proposed. Having interpreted his next utterance, *jubs bread*, as 'birds eating bread', she expands that idea by talking about the birds eating berries, having dinner, their food. Mark plays his part in the conversation too: *Yeh* and *Oh*. He is doing his bit to show that he is participating. We should not read from his responses that he fully understands, of course, but at least he knows the game of conversation and how to play his part in it. All in all, I see this excerpt as being an almost ideal example of language 'teaching' for a child of this age. Though, of course, the mother is not deliberately teaching at all. She is doing what she does quite intuitively, in order to make the conversation interesting and enjoyable for both of them.

This next extract of a recording of Mark was made almost two months later at the age of 25 months. A little earlier in the morning Mark had been looking out of the window watching a man make a bonfire. Now, when he looks again, the man has gone.

Mark is looking out of the kitchen window. Earlier he had seen a man working in his garden.

Mark: Where man gone?
Where man gone?
  M: I don't know
    I expect he's gone inside
    because it's snowing
Mark: Where man gone?
  M: In the house
Mark: Uh?
  M: Into his house
Mark: No
No
Gone to shop Mummy(v)   [The local shop is
  M: Gone where? close to Mark's
     house]

Mark: Gone shop
M: To the shop?
Mark: Yeh
M: What's he going to buy?
Mark: Er – biscuits
M: Biscuits mm
Mark: Uh?
M: Mm
What else?
Mark: Er – meat
M: Mm
Mark: Meat
Er – sweeties
Buy a big bag sweets
M: Buy sweets?
Mark: Yeh
M – er – man – the man
buy sweets
M: Will he?
Mark: Yeh
Daddy buy sweets
Daddy buy sweets
M: Why?
Mark: Oh er – /ə/ shop
Mark do buy some –
sweet – sweeties
Mark buy some – um –
Mark buy some – um –
I did

For a child of just over two, this is a quite remarkable achievement, for it is clearly a story – at least in rudimentary form. It starts with the observation that the man has gone and then builds up quite an elaborate account of where he has gone. No matter that the identity of the principal chacter is somewhat changeable; the achievement is in the development of an idea which draws upon imagined as well as actual experience.

But here too it is the mother's contribution I want to draw attention to. At first glance one might think that she is not actually doing very much – just a few simple questions and acknowledgements. But one can see how those questions provide 'a scaffold', to use Bruner's term (Ninio and Bruner, 1978), within which Mark is able to develop his story. Extending, then, need not always be a case of *the adult* providing new, related information. Sometimes it is more helpful if the adult makes it possible for the child to do this extending him or herself. As here. The result is, as so often in successful adult–child conversation, a joint achievement.

Now, I will contrast that with an extract from another child of exactly the same age conversing with his mother. The topic is different and so, as one can see, is the way in which the conversation goes.

Thomas is in the living room with his mother. There is a plate of biscuits on the table.

T: *biscuits

    M: Those were got specially cos we had visitors at the weekend
Who came to see Tommy?
Who came in a car?

T: See Grannie Irene /ə/ car

    M: Grannie Irene's coming next weekend
But who came last weekend?

T: Auntie Gail in /ə/ train

    M: Auntie Gail's coming
They're coming on the train
yes

T: Colin in /ə/ train

    M: Colin – Colin er – and Anne came in the car didn't they?

T: Colin /ə/ Anne
Colin /ə/ Anne

    M: Yes

T: Colin /ə/ Anne
Colin /ə/ Anne

    M: Colin and Anne came in the train

T: In /ə/ train
Auntie train

    M: No not auntie train darling(v)
Auntie Gail and Grannie Irene are coming on the train on Friday

T: Auntie Gail in /ə/ train
            M: That's right

One can recognize a quite different quality in the conversation here. It comes over in a number of ways. Perhaps the most tell-tale is the mother's intonation. Almost every utterance has a falling tone, the intonation for making independent assertions. It is as if the mother has to put her stamp of approval on everything that Thomas says before it is admitted into the conversation. Also it is the mother who is responsible for the introduction of almost all the topical material into the conversation. One gets the impression that this mother is trying to teach her child not only language, but also about the world, and about truth. But it is only truth according to her view of things that matters, and until the child comes around to her way of thinking then what he says doesn't count.

Now this style of interaction might appear to be well-suited to helping a child to learn to talk, but our results suggest that in fact it is not. At least not for a child of this age. If one has to contrast different styles of language development – and, of course, I'm not claiming that there are only two, nor that these children experience talk like these extracts all the time – but, if one has to try to characterize different styles of talk, then it seems to me that Mark's mother provides a very good example of the supporting and extending style, whilst Thomas's mother seems to be much more dominating and didactic in her approach. And it is Mark, as one can see, who is making the more rapid progress.

But – and this is very important – it must not be forgotten that conversation is a joint activity. Two parties are involved. So, however good the adult's contribution, it will not be effective unless the child plays his or her part. One could say, therefore, that the interesting conversations Mark has with his mother owe as much to Mark as they do to his mother. This, of course, makes life very difficult for us, because it would be so much more convenient if we could think that, if only adults would learn to do things the right way, then all our problems would disappear: children would all learn uniformly rapidly. But, I'm afraid that is not the case. Quite apart from differences in general learning ability, whatever that may prove to be – and general learning ability as applied to language learning probably accounts for quite a lot of the variation between children in rate of development – there seem to be other differences between children which contribute to the rapidity with which they learn to talk. Differences, if you like, of character or temperament, which make some of them much more interesting and rewarding to talk with than others. The result is that these children actually *elicit* the conversational experiences which facilitate their further learning. It seems, then, that the rapid developers are at least partly responsible themselves for the experience that allows them to develop rapidly. Clearly the implications of this view of the reciprocity of interaction are challenging and far-reaching, and I will return to them later when I discuss the school. Before going on to that, though, the following example of a somewhat older child illustrates what the supporting and extending style looks like for a 3½-year-old child. Now I cannot be so specific as to what characteristics of adult speech are associated with rapid progress at this stage because we have not done the necessary detailed analysis. But I can say that the child involved in this extract was a fairly rapid developer in his oral language and certainly very successful when it came to learning to read. The example was recorded when James was 3¾ years old. In it, he was acting out an imaginary train journey with his mother.

James and his mother are in the living room sitting on the sofa, pretending it is a train.

M: There we are
I'll sit on the side
Right . . are you ready?
All set . .
Right . . off with the brake

J: I'll start it up

M: Oh sorry!
Right . .

J: Mum(v) . . . you don't steer it yet

M: Oh . . well

J: (train noises)
                           [J pretends to start the engine]

M: Oh! that was a quick
starting engine
Very good!
Got enough coal at the back?

. . .

Have you shovelled enough coal on James(v)?

J: Yes

M: Good!
Away we go then!
Wave goodbye to your
friends
Right
(engine noises, accelerating)

J: (chuckles)

M: (engine whistle noise)
We're going very fast
now James(v)
. . .
Can you feel the carriages
swaying?

J: Yeh

M: Can you?

J: Yeh

M: Oh they're rolling me about
Oh . . all my breakfast is
rumbling in my tummy
Oh! . . Oh! . . Oh!

J: (engine noises)

M: I think we'll have to slow
down now don't you?

J: Mm (agrees)

M: I think we're going a bit too
fast
. . .
That's better
That's easier now isn't it?

J: Mm (agrees)

M: (hums)
Look at the cows in the field
James(v)

J: Mm

M: And there's a farmer look
The farmer's waving to you

J: Mm

That last extract is, I think, my favourite amongst all the recordings we have made. When you bear in mind that the families had no idea when they were being recorded, I think it is quite remarkable that we have caught a sustained episode like this. Once again it illustrates the way in which the sensitive adult can pick up what a child is currently interested in and enrich and develop the topic, both providing an opportunity for learning language and, as I stated at the beginning, an opportunity for learning through language.

In the pre-school years, then – and, of course, throughout a person's life, but particularly at this time – conversation is most effective when it is collaborative, when it is a joint construction. The adults adjust their speech to the child's level of development. But they also depend upon the child's contributions to make up conversation which provides the scaffolding within which the child constructs his or her own understanding of language and the model of the world that is expressed through language. The expression I would use to characterize what is going on here is *apprenticeship in meaning:* the child, as it were, working with a skilled craftsman and learning by doing alongside that skilled craftsman (*cf.* Vygotsky, 1978).

And so to School

At five, all the children in our study made the transition to school, and unlike the pupil in Shakespeare's soliloquy on the seven ages of man, they all went willingly to school. In fact one of the most pleasant things about observing children at the beginning of infant school is seeing how much they all enjoy it. Which makes it all the more sad that, by the age of 11, a substantial minority have become completely disenchanted and see themselves as low achievers, incapable of making good use of the educational opportunities offered to them.

The question is, why is it that so many children who started off so well, so full of enthusiasm, have become so disenchanted? One widely-held belief is that a major cause of low achievement is 'linguistic disadvantage' and one of the main aims of our follow-up study has been to discover just how far this is a helpful way of looking at the problem.

The term 'linguistic disadvantage' has been used by people working within a number of different theoretical perspectives. Some have held the view that a minority of children come to school with completely inadequate linguistic resources. So often I hear about the large proportion of children entering infant school who are simply non-verbal, who have no language. I can only express my amazement that in other parts of the country there are so many deprived children, because in Bristol, apparently, we do not have such children. (I must say that I also have my doubts about the frequency with which they are found in other parts of the country.) Though I should make it quite clear that the study that we have been engaged in has been concerned only with children who have been judged not to be handicapped in any way, whose parents are native speakers of English, and who have been brought up in their own homes. Now of course that excludes a small minority of children that may indeed contain a number who are non-verbal on entry to school. But from the number that is quoted to me on many occasions ('one-third of my class' is quite a frequent figure mentioned) we are not talking about that small minority of say 2 or 3 per cent of native speakers of English who are seriously handicapped and who were excluded from our study. And of course, I have nothing whatsoever to say about non-native speakers of English. Our study has not been concerned with them and I do not feel I am in a position to make any comments on their problems – though of course such children are no more likely to be non-verbal in their mother tongue than are the children we have been studying. So, talking about normal, native speakers of English, it does not appear to us that there are many – in fact hardly any at all – who come to school with seriously inadequate linguistic resources.

A second perspective on linguistic disadvantage has claimed that dialect differences between homes and schools are responsible for many children's apparent inadequacy in the classroom. Of course I am thinking now particularly of research done in the USA by people like Labov (e.g. Labov, 1970). In our Bristol study we have quite a high proportion of children who speak with a local dialect and with accents which are non-standard to varying degrees. We asked the teachers to assess the extent to which the different children used non-standard English and then we looked at the relationship between the teachers' rating of the children and their academic attainment. What we found was that there was no statistically significant relationship between non-standard dialect at the age of five on entry to school and the children's attainment at age seven. So it appears then that, provided the teachers are prepared to accept dialect differences, this does not provide a problem for the children. I would also refer you to the work which has been done in London by Jim Wight, (1975), who set out to make a study of the problems of West Indian children, in particular those resulting from dialect differences, and very quickly discovered that the West Indian children were bi-dialectal. They were perfectly able to cope with the relatively standard dialect of the classroom, certainly as listeners and as understanders. He concluded that one should not be misled by the fact that their speech is very frequently non-standard. This does not mean they are not able to understand and participate in what is going on in the classroom. In fact his conclusion was that it was the content of the lessons and of the materials they were expected to

learn from that was the problem, not the discrepancy in dialect.
The third perspective that has been taken on linguistic disadvantage claims that the language used in the home is different from the language used in the classroom, both in form and also more specifically in function – the uses that are made of language (e.g. Tough, 1977). Here too we have not really found any very strong evidence of children who are unable to cope with the language demands of the classroom because they are unfamiliar with the ways in which language is used in school. One particular characteristic of classroom talk that might be thought to be unfamiliar to some children is what we have called 'display questions' – that is to say where the adult asks a question to which he or she already knows the answer and the child has – to put it somewhat unkindly – to guess the answer that is in the teacher's mind and, in many cases, to come up with the right formulation of it, down to the precise word. In practice almost all children have been playing this game since the very beginning of language learning. All parents play the game of 'what's that?' and wait for the child to produce the right label. In fact Bruner (Ninio and Bruner, 1978) has shown that this is central to the early stages of language learning, and it continues throughout the pre-school years. So it is not the case that children come to school unfamiliar with the display question sequence. Nor are they unfamiliar with various types of indirect request, such as 'Shall we all come and sit on the rug now?'

Conversation in the Classroom

It seems, therefore, that none of these perspectives offers an entirely satisfactory explanation of how linguistic disadvantage leads to the low educational attainment that is characteristic of many lower-class children, though I agree that each points to what may be a contributory factor and, if all were combined in one child, it might be that such a child would be at a serious disadvantage in comparison with his or her peers.

However, rather than continue to search in the child alone for the attributes that are associated with lack of success, let us adopt a different strategy and turn our attention to the interactions, involving both teacher and pupil, in which the child's ability is assessed. I do not mean tests or formal assessment sessions but simply the ordinary everyday conversation which makes up so large a part of each child's experience of school. Could it be that the 'linguistic disadvantage' that the teacher perceives is, in fact, a product of the manner in which the teacher interacts with the child?

The following evidence is relevant to this question. It is taken from the recordings of Rosie, one of the children in our full longitudinal study. Rosie is the last child in a family of five, the eldest of whom is 11 years old. Until 1979, they lived in a small terrace house in the inner city. Her father has not been employed for at least the last ten years and her mother does not have a job either. The children are clearly materially deprived, though not, to my way of thinking, emotionally deprived. However, in terms of her material and intellectual environment, I suppose Rosie must be one of the most disadvantaged children in our study. She was also the lowest scoring child on the tests administered on entry to school (see Chap. 5).

In the following extract Rosie is at home, talking with her mother a few weeks before she started school.

Rosie comes into the kitchen to tell her mother that she has tidied the front room.

R: Mum(v) I've picked it all up there

M: Have you?
There's a <u>good</u> girl

R: <u>Yes</u>
There ain't no bits in there

M: We got to make the beds later on

R: Uh?

M: Make the beds

R: Come on then

M: Not yet

R: What in a minute?

M: Yeh in a minute

R: What – what time clock have we got to do it?

M: I don't know
I'll see how –
Got to wash up first
What's the time by the clock?

R: Uh?

M: What's the time?
Now what number's that?
[M points to hands on clock]

R: Number two

M: No it's not
What is it?
It's one and a nought

R: One and a nought

M: Yeh
What's one and a nought

R: (no response)

M: What is it?

R: That one

M: Yeh
What is it?

R: One
One and a nought

M: What's one and a nought?

R: Um that

M: Ten!

R: Ten (imitates)

M: Ten to ten

R: Ten to ten (imitates with enthusiasm)
Well shall we wash them because they're not clean enough?

[R refers to numbers on clock]

M: (shakes head)

R: On that other side he ain't (in justification)

M: Well you can't wash him inside
He'd break

R: Would he?

M: Mm (confirming)

R: If – if – if we wash him inside w – wou – wouldn't – w – w – would that thing wouldn't go round?

Well, I am not for a moment claiming that this is an ideal conversational experience. All I want to argue is that it provides strong evidence that Rosie is a reasonably competent user of English. She may not be able to tell the time and her mother may not be going about teaching her in the most effective way, but there is no doubt that Rosie understands a 'display question' and is able to keep her end up and to come back with a topic of her own initiation following the time-telling episode. (Note her quite complex suggestion 'shall we wash them because they're not clean enough?')

About six weeks later, Rosie began to attend the local infant school and she joined a cooperative unit in which two teachers taught some 40 children of varying nationalities and mother tongues. During the course of our morning's observation of Rosie, some six weeks after she had started school, she spent some time interacting with each of the teachers. The comparison is instructive.

In the first example she is with Teacher A, and is engaged in that familiar pre-Christmas activity of cutting out the picture from one of last year's Christmas cards, fastening a calendar on the bottom and so producing a Christmas present for Mum. The picture on Rosie's card shows Father Christmas skiing down a snowy mountainside. Teacher A is trying to talk to Rosie about this picture, though she has to break off for a moment to answer another child, C, who is also demanding her attention.

Rosie is with a small group who are making calendars.

   C: Miss(v) I done it
      T: Will you put it at the top?
   C: Miss(v) I done it
    Look
      T: What are those things? (to R)
       [T points with finger at card]
   C: Miss(v) I done it
    Miss(v) I done it
      [R drops something and picks it up]
      T: What are those things? (to R)
   C: Miss(v) I done it
      T: D'you know what they're called? (referring to objects on card)
R: (shakes head)
      T: What d'you think he uses them for?

R: (looks at card)

    T: It's very nice (to C, referring to her calendar)
    T: After play we'll put some ribbon at the top (to C)

C: What?

    T: Ribbon at the top to hang them up by (to C) Would you put all the cards together now?

. .

    Put the cards together

C: Oh

    T: All right? What's – what are those? (to R)

. . . . .

    What d'you think he uses them for?

    [R rubs one eye]

R: Go down –

    T: Go down – ? Yes you're right Go on

. .

    [R rubs both eyes]
    What's the rest of it?
    [T puts down card]
    You have a little think and I'll get – er get the little calendar for you

. .

    I think you're sitting on one
    [T points to it and R picks it up]
    ‹Right› could you put some glue on the back there?

. .

    He uses those to go down – ?

. . . . .

    Is it a hill or a mountain?

R: A hill

    T: A hill yes
    And what's on the hill?

R: Ice

    T: Yes ice
    They're called skis

C: Miss(v) –
(Interruption while T deals with other children)
[T returns to R]
    T: That's lovely
    And after play we'll
    put some ribbon –
    What do you think the
    ribbon's for?

R: For Father Christmas

    T: For Father Christmas?
    [T straightens up
    and looks at the
    card, pointing]
    T: If I – you want to put
    it up on the wall you
    have a little piece of
    ribbon long enough to
    hang it up by

If this were one's first observation of Rosie, one might be forgiven for thinking that she had a serious language deficit. And yet from her dialogue with her mother at home, we know she has not. What is it that is happening here, then? The answer, I think, is that, because Teacher A fails to establish a relationship of conversational *reciprocity* with her, Rosie is not given an opportunity to contribute in a way that is meaningful to *her*. However, as one could hear in her voice, this is not because the teacher is lacking in concern. On the contrary, she is so anxious to get Rosie to produce an answer that she can work on somehow or other, that Rosie is, as it were, squeezed out and she therefore *appears* to be incompetent.

Later in the same morning Rosie spent some time with the other teacher. On this occasion the task was reading, and Rosie was reading from a little book in which each sentence has the form 'I am tall said the . . .'

Rosie is reading to Teacher B from *I am Tall*. Another child is with her.

Talking and Learning 23

R: I am tall said the – tower

T: Chimney

R: Chimbley

T: It's a big factory chimney isn't it?
[T points at the picture]

R: I don't like –

T: There's a lot of smoke coming out of the top

R: I don't like that one
[R points at the picture]

T: You don't like it?

R: (shakes head)

T: Why not?

R: I only likes little ones

T: Have you got a chimney in your house?

R: (nods emphatically)

C: And me

T: D'you have smoke coming out of the top?

R: (nods emphatically)

T: Mm?

R: (nods again)

[T turns page then closes book]

T: What's underneath the chimney then that makes the smoke come out?

C: I know – fire

T: Mm? (to R)

R: Fire

T: Is it?
Is that a fire then?

C: Miss(v) can I have this one?

T: Which room's the fire in? (to R)
Yes (to C)

R: In the front one

T: Is it?
So it keeps you warm
Lovely

R: And I got a bed

R: 'e's upstairs

R: Carol got a bed and Kelvin . . . and Carol

R: Donna – we're sharing it

R: (nods emphatically)

R: Yeh an I –
When I gets up I creeps in Mummy's bed

T: Where's your bed?

T: Anybody else got a bed in your room?

T: Um hum
What about Donna?

T: You're sharing with Donna are you?

T: Do you have a cuddle at night?

T: For another cuddle?
Ooh that's nice
It's nice in the morning when you cuddle

If *this* had been one's first observation of Rosie, one would have formed an altogether different impression of her. Here she appears to be alert and vivacious, willing not only to offer her opinions, but to initiate a topic and to develop it.

Since Rosie is the same child in both extracts, the difference in her performance cannot be attributed to her. It must be the result of the style of interaction adopted by the two different teachers and of the way in which Rosie perceived the expectations of the tasks in which the two teachers attempted to engage her. Teacher A, by insisting that Rosie should construe the picture of Father Christmas from her own, *teacher-like* perspective, made her feel inadequate. By contrast, Teacher B, in encouraging Rosie to develop her personal response to the picture of the chimney, gives her a chance to talk about a subject on which she is an expert – her own home – and thereby obtains a much more positive estimation of Rosie's linguistic ability.

At this point, if one recalls the two earlier examples of mother-child conversation, I do not think it is too difficult to see a parallel between Teacher B and Mark's mother, on the one hand, and Teacher A and Thomas's mother on the other. And I would suggest that the supporting and extending strategy that is so beneficial for a two-year-old is equally beneficial for a five-year-old, particularly when, like Rosie, that five-year-old has not had the advantage of a great deal of that sort of experience in the years before coming to school.

What I am arguing, then, is that the so-called 'linguistic disadvantage' of children like Rosie is to a considerable extent the result of the inappropriate interactional situation they are placed in. For such children, in particular, a sharp transition to a teacher-dominated, interrogation-like style of interaction is likely to lead to a loss of confidence and a feeling of inadequacy, from which they may never fully recover. And in this way a teacher's low expectation may indeed become a self-fulfilling prophecy.

With such children it is more than ever necessary to 'start where the child is'. And that means being prepared to listen and to let the child talk about that which he or she is interested in and knowledgeable about. Once the necessary confidence and trust has been established, it will be possible to introduce new information and to ask questions that require the child to think more critically and systematically.

But it is not only with the more immature pupils that a more reciprocal, negotiating style of interaction is desirable. It is my belief that all of us learn more effectively when we are allowed to play a larger part in selecting the tasks we engage in and in deciding how they should be carried out. Our research shows that this is true of the pre-schooler, and my own experience has convinced me that it is equally true for teachers on advanced courses. Surely it is equally true for the years of schooling in between: that the most effective learning takes place when the learner is engaged on a task or problem which is formulated in terms of his or her own purposes and understanding, rather than on a task that is imposed from without.

If we want the children of today to grow up with the confidence and competence to meet the demands for critical, adaptive and creative thinking that the years ahead will certainly make of the society to which we all belong, it is essential that we should encourage these qualities from the very beginning. Let me conclude, therefore, by suggesting that, at school as well as at home, the most effective talking and learning will take place when adult and child engage together collaboratively in the *negotiation of meaning*.

CHAPTER 2
A Naturalistic Approach to the Study of Language Development

During the last half-century, children's language development has been studied for a variety of different reasons – to provide age-related norms of performance (Templin, 1957; Loban, 1963); as a basis for assessment and remediation (Lee, 1970; Crystal *et al.*, 1976); to chart the stages through which children pass in achieving mastery of the adult language (Brown *et al.*, 1969); and to provide supporting evidence for theories of cognitive development (Piaget, 1926) and of socialization (Bernstein, 1971) – and the methods that have been employed have been dependent, at least in part, upon the larger goals of the research. But almost all these researchers have made some use of naturalistic observations. The longitudinal research that we are engaged on in Bristol under the general title of 'Language at Home and at School', has affinities with most of the examples referred to above, and also makes substantial use of naturalistic speech data.

The aims of our research are fourfold:

1. to provide a normative description of linguistic ability at regular intervals between 1¼ and 5 years;
2. to describe the sequence of emergence of certain aspects of the language system, and to discover how far this sequence is invariant across children;
3. to seek to identify factors in the children's environment that are causative of rapid or slow development;
4. to explain the contribution of pre-school language experience to successful adjustment and learning in the first two years of formal schooling.

A variety of research techniques is being employed to achieve these aims, including exploratory and standardized tests and interviews with parents and teachers (see Chap. 5 for further details), but central amongst these is the collection and analysis of samples of spontaneous speech, and it is to a description and discussion of this approach that this chapter will be devoted.

A Naturalistic Approach to the Study of Language Development

Sampling Spontaneous Speech

Communication through language is an exceedingly complex form of behaviour and one that is often cited as distinguishing us from all other species. Because it is so complex, however, the temptation is to focus on just one aspect of it, in an attempt to gain a better purchase, ignoring what is recalcitrant to inclusion within the theory; unfortunately what is gained in precision with respect to the aspect focused on is frequently lost in distortions introduced into the conception of the whole. The history of linguistics and of psycho- and sociolinguistics over the last 50 years bears witness to the difficulty of maintaining a sense of proportion, as one partial point of view has been succeeded by another. Nevertheless, although sometimes highly technical and apparently far removed from the speech that takes place in the home, the school or the market place, the arguments of the theoreticians are of considerable importance to those studying the development of language, for the domain of the latter's inquiries will depend to a considerable extent on the theory of language that they espouse, and their results, in turn, can provide evidence crucial to deciding between competing linguistic theories (Chomsky, 1965).

How then should one conceptualize what it is that children have to acquire as they learn their native language?

The approach that we adopted in 1972, when we started our research, was to be as comprehensive as possible in drawing upon available theories, and to define the task very broadly as 'the acquisition of the ability to communicate through language in situationally contextualised conversation'. Much of our effort over the last few years has been devoted to filling out the detail of that rather programmatic definition, first by attempting to describe the linguistic communication of mature speakers, and then by relating this to what is known about the context in which this ability is acquired (Wells, 1975a,b, 1976).

To summarize the arguments there presented, we see linguistic communication as one form of purposeful, interpersonal behaviour, which has acquired its importance and ubiquity because of the relative precision with which it allows individuals to share in each other's experience and endeavours. This is achieved by the sender constructing a particular meaning configuration, consisting of 'purpose', 'topic' and 'affect' and encoding it into a conventional rule-governed sequence of linguistic forms which can be given physical realization through speech or writing. Receivers, for their part, provided they are members of the same cultural and linguistic community, are able to draw upon their own past experience to form expectations concerning the probable content and form of the message in order to match these with their decoding of the actual signal, and thus to construct for themselves a meaning that approximates quite closely to that intended by the sender.

Learning a first language is thus essentially learning to make a match between the linguistic forms used in a culture and one's internalized organization of experience in that culture. Put very simply, it seems that in learning to comprehend the speech of others, the task of children is to make the match between the meanings that they can expect in well-understood contexts and the linguistic forms of utterances that are addressed to them in such contexts, whilst in learning to speak, on the other hand, their task is to select from their existing repertoire the forms that best express the meaning that they intend and to combine those forms into temporally-organized, socially-acceptable utterances. Patient, interested interlocutors, who are prepared to help them achieve the match between meaning–intention and form seem likely to be essential for the child's progress, and the medium through which the skills are acquired to be normal, everyday conversation.

Given this view of language and its development, we believe that the primary data for study must be samples of the child's spontaneous verbal interaction, and over the last three years we have made more than 1,280 recordings of naturally occurring conversation in children's homes, and we are currently engaged in analysing them.

However, samples of spontaneous behaviour also have limitations. Children's systematic knowledge of language at any stage can never be fully represented in the particular instances of behaviour that are called forth by the contexts in which they find themselves (Ingram, 1969), and so there is the problem of how to make inferences about potential from the limited sample of actual behaviour that is recorded. This limitation has been most strongly urged by Chomsky, who considers samples of spontaneous speech to be almost worthless and argues that research on language development 'must be carried out in devious and clever ways, if any serious result is to be obtained' (1964, p.36).

With older children and adults it is possible to devise procedures that tap this systematic knowledge, by asking subjects to evaluate the grammaticality or acceptability of particular forms, but such a reflective, metalinguistic attitude to language is quite slow to develop, and young children's responses to such investigations can be quite bizarre. For example, in reply to the question 'Which is right, "two shoes" or "two shoe"?', Adam, one of Brown's subjects, replied with explosive enthusiasm 'Pop goes the weasel!' (Brown and Bellugi, 1964, p.136).

One of the reasons for the difficulty experienced in using such techniques with young children, a difficulty which also afflicts most language tests, is that the language behaviour they call for is artificially divorced from a meaningful context in the child's experience and is thus not appropriate evidence for the question under investigation, namely, the child's ability to use language to communicate with those around him or her. To put it differently, to be able to use language effectively in conversation, it is not necessary to be able to make conscious judgements about other people's use of language out of context. At the present time, therefore, we believe that samples of actual language use still provide the most trustworthy evidence, even though attended by problems to which there is no easy solution.

One particular problem concerns the representativeness of the speech sample recorded. What people say is to a considerable extent dependent on the activity involved, who they are talking to, and how much in the way of shared knowledge and attitudes they can take for granted; and this is also true of children. Most infant teachers know of children who are monosyllabic in the classroom, but amusing raconteurs in the playground, such as the black child, Larry, studied by Labov (1970). Sampling in one situation only, therefore, may yield a picture of a child's ability which seriously distorts the overall reality in ways which it is difficult to estimate. One solution, of course, is systematically to sample from a number of predetermined situations, but this too is somewhat artificial, particularly in the case of very young children. Our own solution has been to equip the children with radio-microphones, which they wear all day, and to take a large number of short samples at frequent intervals, in the belief that the total corpus of conversation collected in this way is least likely to misrepresent the variety of situations in which language is used during the course of a typical day.

A further issue affecting representativeness is whether or not to have an observer present during the recording. Here one is on the horns of a dilemma. The younger the child, the more dependent his or her speech is on the support of the specific context and on gestural communication. Many utterances are indeed uninterpretable without such situational information, and it requires an observer or camera to record the necessary information. However, unless the observer is also the parent, as is frequently the case in intensive studies of individual children such as those by Clark (1974) and Halliday (1975), the presence of either of these outside agencies inevitably affects the behaviour of the conversational participants being observed, and this is particularly serious when one is attempting to discover what a child's normal experience of language is like. An example of the distorting effect of an observer can be found in an early paper by Roger Brown (Brown and Bellugi, 1964), who was led to argue for the importance of what he called 'expansions' on the basis of their relatively high incidence in the speech samples that his research team recorded on their visits to children's homes. In contrast, our own research technique, which does not make use of an observer, has produced little evidence of maternal utterances which could be described as expansions, except when another adult who is unfamiliar with the child is present. Under these circumstances, however, the mother quite frequently expands the child's utterance, but apparently more to make the child's meaning intelligible to the other adult than to provide a model for the child. Of course, some valuable contextual information is lost by dispensing with on-the-spot observation, and our method of playing over the recording to the mother at the end of the day and asking her to recall the context and activity of each episode does not capture all the relevant details; but we believe that this is a necessary price to pay for uncontaminated samples of spontaneous conversation from children spanning a wide range of family backgrounds.

Transcription

Before recorded speech is analysed, it is usual to make a written transcript, which then forms the basis for subsequent work. This task is not without problems, although they are not very different from those experienced, albeit at a level below conscious awareness, by the participants in a conversation. The aim is clear – to produce a completely accurate account of what was said, particularly by the child; unfortunately one can never know when this has been achieved. In fact, because of the nature of linguistic communication, there can never be absolute certainty about what has been said, only extremely well-motivated guesses, which are usually corroborated by subsequent contributions to the conversation. However, misunderstandings do occur, and these may be due either to errors of articulation or of selection and sequencing of units of the utterance by the speaker, of which they may not even be aware, or to errors introduced by the listener, who, in actively scanning the incoming signal to achieve a match, may mishear or be misled by their own expectations into an interpretation, which although plausible to them, is at odds with the speaker's intentions. However, in adult conversations such misunderstandings are usually corrected or compensated for as the

A Naturalistic Approach to the Study of Language Development 31

dialogue continues and new light is cast, retrospectively, on earlier utterances. In conversations in which a young child is one of the participants, on the other hand, uncertainty about what was said is more common, and it is also more likely to remain unresolved.

If it is difficult for the participants in a conversation to be certain about what was said, it is even more difficult for a transcriber to achieve certainty, when he or she was not a party to the conversation and does not have the concomitant situational and gestural information. This is particularly so when background noise rises above the level of the speaker's voice, as inevitably happens from time to time with naturalistic recordings. A certain proportion of utterances, therefore, are bound to be problematic, giving rise to a variety of alternative interpretations. With adults, it is often possible to ask for confirmation of a particular interpretation when making the transcription, but with the utterances of young children this is not possible, and there is no alternative but to accept either the transcriber's or the mother's interpretation of the utterance, arrived at after the event. The transcriber has the advantage of being able to listen to the utterance over and over again, and, where the context allows strong expectations to be formed about probable messages, this may lead to a relatively certain interpretation, but there is always the danger that the transcriber's theoretical preconceptions will introduce bias. The mother, on the other hand, has the double advantage of having been a participant in the conversation, and of knowing the child's interests and habits and his or her idiosyncratic speech forms; unless her interpretation can be shown to be wrong, therefore, it is likely to be the more acceptable.

Of course, mothers do make mistakes, and sometimes these are vigorously rejected by the child himself, as in the following example:

Mark is looking out of the window. Mother is in the same room, reading.

Mark: A man – er – dig. .
       down there
                       M: A man walked down
                            there? (checking)
Mark: Yeh
                       M: Oh yes
                         . . 8 . .
Mark: A man's fire Mummy(v)   [Mk sees the man is
                                        making a bonfire]
                       M: Mm?

Mark: A man's fire

    M: Mummy's flower? (checking)

Mark: No

    M: What?

Mark: Mummy(v)
The man . fire (clearly articulating each word)

    M: Man's fire? (checking)

Mark: Yeh

    M: Oh yes the bonfire

Mark: Bonfire

However, since successful communication can and does take place between mother and child, one must assume that her interpretations are correct more often than not. In the early stages, indeed, it is the very fact of putting an interpretation on children's utterances that is important, for it is in this way that they discover initially that their vocalizations have meaning and then, gradually, through the feedback provided by the mother's responses, what precise meaning they have. In an important sense, they do not know precisely what they mean, until they hear, not what they say, as in the case of the proverbial old woman, but what other people say in response.

Thus whether by mother or by transcriber, or better still by both in collaboration, the interpretation of a child's utterances must rely quite heavily on intuition derived from experience. It is worth stressing this point since earlier studies, which were not theoretically concerned with meaning, tended to gloss over this interpretative aspect of their methodology, priding themselves on their empirical rigour in describing only the observable, or 'surface' level of language behaviour. As I hope that I have shown, there can be no description without prior interpretation, and this must inevitably be open to error.

A final problem at the stage of transcription concerns the relation between spoken and written language. For convenience, transcripts are usually made in standard orthography, with the addition of a number of diacritics. But this fails to capture certain significant dimensions of the meaning conveyed by spoken utterances. The systematic contrasts of intonation can be rendered in some form of notation (see p.38 below for an example), but qualities such as pace and tone of voice are very much more difficult to represent (Crystal, 1975) and the most satisfactory solution at present seems to be a parenthetical gloss.

Producing an accurate and informative transcription is not a problem that is unique to research on language development, however, for achieving accuracy and reliability in recording observations presents difficulties in all the social sciences that attempt to segment the stream of behaviour into theoretically meaningful units. In many cases, inter-observer reliability is bought at the expense of arbitrariness in the categories employed, and there is usually a residue of uncodable segments. In transcribing speech, one feels, this should not have to be the case, for the fact that writing systems provide a complete and systematic representation of certain aspects of linguistic behaviour tends to obscure the relative indeterminacy of a considerable part of the stream of speech. However, the goal of complete accuracy can no more be attained in this branch of the behavioural sciences than it can in any other; it is only our much greater understanding of the systematic nature of language behaviour that renders the occurrence of error more salient.

Coding and Analysis

The transcript of the recording, once produced and checked, provides the basis for the subsequent stages of description and analysis. Here the researcher can have a number of aims, and almost all of them will require a coding operation in which the particular utterances and their constituent parts are assigned to theoretical categories, and here again many of the problems of interpretation already discussed arise in an even stronger form. In developmental studies, what one is trying to discover is the gradual development of the child's knowledge of the principles underlying utterances to the stage where they operate in an adult-like manner. Clearly one cannot question children about their knowledge, and so one has to rely upon inferences from those utterances that do, and those that do not, occur. There is a further problem in that the occurrence of a particular pattern is not in itself evidence that the child controls the corresponding rule in the adult grammar: Ruth Clark (1975) has shown that some, if not all, children utilize a strategy of incorporating 'ready-made chunks' from previously heard utterances without analysing their internal structure. The task, then, is to describe as accurately as possible the principles of construction that the child is actually using productively at any particular stage.

In our research, we are trying to achieve this by keeping the coding of the pragmatic, semantic and syntactic aspects of each child utterance relatively independent, so that the relationship between them can be treated as a matter for investigation. Under the pragmatic heading, we code each child utterance with respect to the context in which it occurs, the purpose of the conversation of which it is a part, and the function that it specifically performs in that conversation. In addition, the functions of preceding and following utterances by other speakers are coded, as are the appropriateness of fit between consecutive utterances. The semantic coding describes the state or event that is the topic of the utterance, and the temporal, aspectual, modal and manner modifications of that state or event. The way in which the information in the utterance is arranged to fit its textual context is then described in terms of voice, thematic organization and cohesion. Finally the actual surface syntax of the utterance is described as a linear sequence of constituents structured in a hierarchy of levels. A typical utterance requires somewhere between 50 and 100 separate codings. (The full coding scheme can be found in the Project *Coding Manual* (Wells, 1975c).)

The normative description, for specific age-points, which is one of the goals of our research, can be made relatively simply from these coded data by counting, with the assistance of a computer, the frequency of occurrence of specific categories and sub-categories. So, for example, we can say what proportion of children's utterances, at a particular age, have the function of question, or refusal of a command; what proportion contain multi-clausal structures; what proportion contain auxiliary verbs, and so on. We can also describe the distribution of utterances with these characteristics in relation to demographic variables such as sex, class of family background, position in family, etc.

The same coded data, viewed longitudinally, also provide the basis for investigations of the sequence in which control of the language system is acquired. We are particularly interested, for example, in the acquisition of the auxiliary verb system, which has particular importance in English as it is involved in the expression of the semantic categories of time and aspect, as well as of the pragmatic functions of questioning and modulating the direct form of commands through requests, suggestions, etc. The general question is whether there is, as seems probable, any order in which different distinctions are acquired: for example, are the semantic categories of 'permission' and 'ability' both realized at approximately the same stage? and are modal verbs, such as 'can' and 'must', acquired at the same stage as the morphological forms which mark continuous (v-ing), and perfect (v-ed), aspect? The way in which we are attempting to answer these questions is by searching each child's longitudinal record for occurrences of the categories in question and tabulating their frequency on each occasion of recording. The number of children for whom 'permission' and 'ability', for example, are both realized for the first time on one particular occasion can then be compared with the number for whom one preceded the other, and a conclusion drawn about the acceptability of the original hypothesis.

The main problem here is in deciding what frequency of occurrence on any one occasion of recording is to count as evidence for the acquisition of a particular distinction. A single occurrence might well be considered inadequate, particularly since the item in question might occur as part of a rote-learned sequence or be an imitation of a previous speaker's utterance. On the other hand, the item might have a very low frequency of occurrence in the language as a whole, and to set a criterion of more than one occurrence in 100 utterances would be seriously to reduce the likelihood of attributing mastery where this was justified. Unfortunately no baseline statistics exist for the frequency with which linguistic distinctions occur in the language as a whole, and even if they did they would offer little guidance on the frequencies that could be expected in the speech of pre-school children. However, the normative descriptions at selected age-points, described above, will go some way to providing such baselines for our particular sample of children, and this information will help us to set appropriate frequency criteria. In coming to a decision in any particular instance, two further considerations need to be taken into account. The first is the number of alternatives in the system from which the choice is made, where such a choice is mandatory: for example, in the time-reference system, there are only three possibilities, and so a relatively high criterion frequency can be set, whilst, in comparison, more than 50 alternatives are recognized for the category of sentence meaning relation, and this demands that a very low criterion be set, if the less common alternatives are to be picked up at all. The second is consistency over consecutive recordings: if a category occurs in all subsequent recordings after its first occurrence, even at a very low frequency level, a decision to attribute mastery on the first occasion is more likely to be correct than an attribution based on a high frequency on a particular occasion followed by a complete absence on a number of subsequent occasions before its eventual reappearance in a more stable form.

A third form of analysis in which the coded speech data can be utilized is in the search for environmental factors that may be causative of rapid or slow development. Such investigations have tended in the past to be limited to social or demographic variables, social class, in particular, frequently being cited as the most significant environmental factor. However, our own results to date suggest that when one studies a sample of children that is representative of the full social spectrum, as opposed to one which accentuates the two extremes, much smaller correlations are obtained. But the more important criticism of such an approach is that, whatever the size of the correlations, they cannot explain the nature of the relationship. As we have argued, family membership of any social group cannot of itself be considered to determine the course of a child's linguistic development; the effect, if there is one, must be mediated by the actual patterns of interaction through which the values and orientations of different groups are given realization and acquired by the child. In addition to considering demographic variables, therefore, we have attempted to measure other aspects of the children's environments that reflect more directly the quality of the verbal interactions which they experience, and which can be considered as more direct determinants of success in language development. It is for this reason that the speech of others that provides the context for the children's utterances is also coded with respect to the major pragmatic and semantic categories.

Analyses to test hypotheses about the effect of environmental factors, such as, for example, the frequency with which the child's utterances are confirmed or corrected, as appropriate, requires a different approach from that described above. Here the basic procedure is the analysis of correlation between the rank order of the children on some index of linguistic ability, and a rank order of the same children based on the frequency of utterances of specific kinds addressed to them on previous occasions. An important issue here concerns the index selected to represent the children's linguistic ability. It has been a common practice to use mean length of utterance (MLU) calculated over all the utterances recorded during a particular time-interval as such an index (McCarthy, 1930, 1954), but a number of researchers have recently cast doubt on the validity of such a measure, and it is clear that after approximately three years of age the tendency for MLU to increase with increasing mastery of the language system is counteracted by a developing tendency for utterances to become more elliptical and syntactically condensed to meet conversational demands for succintness. In a recent comparison of various indices (Wells, 1978a), we found that control of the auxiliary verb system and range of semantic modifications of the clause were sensitive indices for the 3–3½ years age-range, and we plan to identify similar more specific indices that are appropriate for other age-ranges.

A Naturalistic Approach to the Study of Language Development

The Transition from Home to School

The use of spontaneous speech data has been described so far only in relation to recordings that we have made in the children's homes, but we intend to continue our research into the early years of schooling using similar methods of data collection and analysis. A considerable amount of debate has taken place in recent years on the question of 'linguistic disadvantage' and its putative effect on educational success, and large scale intervention programmes have been set up, particularly in the United States, to combat this malaise. Although strong arguments have been advanced both by those who see the problem in terms of a language 'deficit' and by those who see it in terms of language 'difference', very little empirical evidence is available to show that 'linguistic disadvantage' is a significant independent factor in educational failure, and even less that indicates the nature of this disadvantage. There are two ways in which we believe that the study of spontaneous speech can contribute evidence relevant to this debate. First, by following some of the children in our sample through the first two years of schooling, recording samples of their typical linguistic interaction in school, we hope to find out the extent to which this differs from their pre-school experience of linguistic interaction at home, and whether such differences, if they occur, are related to the children's success in school. Secondly, we intend to carry out retrospective comparisons between the children in the sample who are found to contrast in school success, in an attempt to identify characteristics, if any, of pre-school linguistic experience which are associated with differential success in school.

The Analysis of Linguistic Interaction

One limitation of all the analyses that we and most other researchers have carried out so far of samples of spontaneous speech is that they are limited to scores summarizing discrete features of individual utterances. But, as was stressed at the beginning of this chapter, utterances normally occur within larger units of interaction, and their meaning and form are partly determined by the negotiation of purpose and topic that characterizes most normal conversation. It seems likely therefore that the way in which children's habitual conversational partners, usually mothers, pick up and, in various ways, develop the stated and implied meanings of their utterances and help them to respond to their utterances in like manner is likely to have a strong influence on the development of their ability to use their command of the language system to contribute effectively to conversation and that this, in turn, will further develop their command of the system. Our future programme will therefore be directed to achieving a more systematic understanding of the ways in which conversation is organized and of the opportunities that participation in conversation provides to become a competent user of language.

An example, which consists of a 90-second sample taken from one of our recordings, will help to illustrate what we intend to focus upon. It also indicates how important a role intonation plays in interaction. (The transcript conventions are given in Appendix 1.)

Jacqueline is playing with the laundry. Mother is washing up.

1 //24→LAUNdry 'bag//   [J has the laundry bag]
2 //35→LAUNdry 'bag//
   . .
3 //In 14 THERE//

4 // ↑ 'Put all . THINGS in//   [J is putting washing in the bag]
5 // ↓ I'm 'putting 35 THINGS in//
6   //24 NO 53 DARling (v) //
7   //'No ↑ 'no ↑ ↑ no 15 NO// ('accel.')
   . . 4 . .
8 // ↑ 'I want to ↑ ↑ 'put those 12 THINGS// ('accel.')
9   //33 YES//
10   //When 'they're 24 WASHED you' can//
11   //'Not 24 beFORE//
   . . .
12 //What's 24 THAT 54 MUM (v)?//
                                  (no response)
   . . 4 . .
13 *//→'You 'dirty 45 CAT// (to baby Jane)
14   Oh she's not
   (laughs)
15   She's not a dirty cat
16   Are you darling (v)? (to baby Jane)

A Naturalistic Approach to the Study of Language Development 39

17		No (command to J)
18		Leave Mummy's washing alone please (firmly)
19		Mummy's got to wash all that
20	//'Wash 243 LINda's –//	[An Auntie Linda gave J some socks and she now refers to them as Linda's socks]
21	There's my socks	
22		***
23	//14 LINda 'bought// some 34 <u>SOCKS 54 MUM</u> (v)//	
24		<u>Yes there</u>'s your socks
25	Lin-	
26		Mummy's washing them
27		I've got to do all that now
28	//25 LINda 'bought you//45 SOCKS 54 MUM(v)//	
29		Yes
30		Linda bought you socks
31		They're dirty
32		They've got to be washed
33	Did. Linda bought ‹you› me got . <u>washed</u>? ('false-starts') (= have the socks Linda bought me got to be washed?) (Trying to repeat Mother's words)	
34		<u>Pardon</u>?
35	//24 LINda wa-//324 WASH them// ('self-correction')	
36		//24 NO//
37		//35 MUMmy's 'going to 'wash them//
38	//15 LINda 'wash them//	
39		//24 NO// 'Linda's 35 NOT 'going to 'wash them//
40	//24 LINda 'not 'going//54 WASH them//	
41		//35 NO//
42		//35 MUMmy 'wash them//
43	//'This is ↑ Daddy's 43 SOCKS 'Mum (v)//	
44		Pardon?
45	//'This is 35 DADdy's 'sock//	

In the first episode (utterances 1–11) Jacqueline is playing with the laundry whilst her mother is washing the dishes. As Jacqueline begins to put the clothes back into the laundry bag, she comments on her activity for her own benefit, and then to share her interest with her mother. Mother turns to answer Jacqueline's attempt to interact, but, when she realizes what Jacqueline is doing, her own intentions concerning the laundry lead her to cut across Jacqueline's intentions with a series of prohibitions (6 – 7) delivered in such a manner, with rising intonation and increasing pace, as to act as a vocal substitute for physical curtailment of Jacqueline's activity. After a pause, Jacqueline reaffirms her own intention (8), repeating Mother's rising pitch and increasing pace with a similar intention to stop Mother interfering with her activity. Mother replies by recognizing the validity of Jacqueline's intention (9–11) and stating the conditions under which she will be permitted to carry it out. At the same time she implies a temporal sequence of events in which Jacqueline's intended activity would be appropriate at one stage rather than another. What is significant here for Jacqueline's learning, we believe, is that her mother, although irritated by Jacqueline's activity, attempts to take account of Jacqueline's intentions as well as her own, in the way in which she verbally controls Jacqueline's behaviour.

Later within the same extract (20–42) there is another episode in which Jacqueline and Mother attempt to understand each other's perception of part of their shared situation. Once again, intonation plays a major role in identifying the aspect of the situation to be focused on, and in negotiating an agreed interpretation. Jacqueline has seen a pair of her socks waiting to be washed and recalls that they have been given to her by Auntie Linda. She tries to share all this information with Mother (33), but has difficulty in organizing the form of her utterance to encode her meaning intention with the right information focus. Following a request for repetition, Jacqueline attempts (35) to express her observation in a simpler form, but, as the hiatus suggests, still has difficulty. The arrangements of the components 'Linda', 'wash' and 'them' (=socks) in the utterance she produces encodes a simple Agent Act on Object clause, in which 'Linda' is the Agent. But this does not correspond with the situation, nor as far as one can judge with Jacqueline's intention. The problem seems to result from a conflict between two intentions: the first is to ask for confirmation of the proposition that the socks are to be washed; the second is to focus attention on the fact that it was Linda who gave her the socks. But having reduced the topic, 'socks', to the status of the anaphoric pronoun 'them', she can no longer qualify it by means of a relative clause in which 'Linda' as Agent could be given information focus. In 36 and 37, Mother rejects Jacqueline's statement as inaccurate and, using marked tonic placement, offers a contrasting true statement, which matches the surface form of Jacqueline's utterance. Jacqueline seems unable to accept this way of putting it and in 38 reaffirms her original formulation, using contrasting marked tonic placement. Mother again rejects Jacqueline's statement, and this time explicitly negates it (39). In 40, Jacqueline, using marked tonic placement, restates her understanding of the fact that it is not *Linda* who is going to wash the socks, and signals her wish for confirmation of this statement. Mother confirms the correctness of Jacqueline's negative statement and (41–42), picking up the contrastive implication of the tonic placement in Jacqueline's utterance, restates the situation positively with 'Mummy' as Agent. Finally, Jacqueline's silence can be taken as agreement with this jointly constructed description of the situation.

These two episodes only have to be compared with a somewhat similar extract from the recording of another child (Appendix 2) to see what widely differing contexts for learning, both about language and about interaction through language, are provided by the normal everyday conversation that children experience in their pre-school years. It is in differences of this sort that we believe an explanation of the effect of language on educational success, if there is one, is likely to be found.

Conclusion

The aim of this chapter has been to describe the way in which we use samples of spontaneous conversation, systematically collected, to describe and explain children's developing ability to communicate through language. However, since linguistic interaction also provides the medium through which a great deal of other learning takes place, speech samples of the kind that we have collected can also provide data for investigations of other kinds. For example, Raban (1975) has explored the contribution of linguistic interaction to a child's developing concept of self, using the longitudinal records of a small sample of the children, and Moon (1976) has investigated the relationship between children's imaginative use of language and subsequent success in learning to read. Other investigations are in progress concerning the antecedents of mathematical knowledge and the development of metalinguistic awareness.

In spite, therefore, of the problems attendant on the use of spontaneous speech data, some of which are quite serious as has been indicated above, we believe that this method has the supreme advantage of allowing one to study the actual process of learning in action, and from a careful analysis of the context, both verbal and situational, to identify the ways in which differing environments can help or hinder this process.

CHAPTER 3
Enabling Factors in Adult–Child Discourse

The use of a special baby-talk register by adults when talking to children in the early stages of language development is now well established (e.g. Sachs, 1977; Snow, 1976), but it is not yet clear how far the specific form it takes in particular adult–child interactions is the result of adult responsiveness to specific communicative abilities of the individual child rather than a generalized response to a less-than-competent interlocutor (Brown, 1977). Newport, *et al.* (1977) found little evidence of mothers adjusting their speech in accordance with their children's growing competence and they argued that, rather than being responsive to characteristics of the child, 'motherese' occurs in response to communication pressures in the situation. Their study, however, concentrated on syntactic characteristics of mother's speech. In contrast, Cross (1977), who investigated a much wider range of maternal speech characteristics, found that, although there was little evidence of adjustment at the level of sentence structure, there was strong evidence of the mothers tuning their input to the child's linguistic ability at the discourse level (i.e. in the manner in which various interpersonal functions were handled in continuous speech). Cross also suggested that the form that fine-tuning takes is likely to vary from one period of development to another, although this is not an issue which has yet been systematically investigated.

Just as the evidence for fine-tuning is not entirely clear, so there is uncertainty regarding which aspects of the child's behaviour are attended to by the adult. Cross found that mothers responded to the children's receptive capacities rather than to the length or grammatical complexity of their speech production. Newport *et al.* suggested that mothers respond to cognitive factors which they take to underlie the children's attention span and processing abilities.

A further question, which has interested many investigators, is the role of adult adjustments in facilitating children's language development. As Newport *et al.* (*op. cit.*) point out, it is one thing to find evidence of the occurrence of 'motherese' and quite another to demonstrate that it has any influence on the course or rate of the child's development. Their own results led them to be quite sceptical of any very general such influence and, although the children who received finely-tuned input in Cross's (1977) study were also fast developers, she was not able, because of the strongly biased nature of her sample, to generalize her findings to all children. In order to overcome this limitation, she carried out a second study (Cross, 1978) to investigate the maternal input to two groups of two-year-old children who differed in their rate of development. The speech of the mothers of the two groups was not observed to differ substantially at the grammatical level, but mothers of the accelerated developers were observed to use a greater proportion of repetitions, fewer wholly or partially unintelligible utterances, fewer utterances per conversational turn and also sentences which were less complex with regard to those grammatical components which occurred before the main verb.

Although it is tempting to interpret these observed differences between the two groups of mothers in Cross's study as evidence of fine-tuning and the difference in rate of development between the two groups of children as the result of this fine-tuning, this is not really warranted, as the estimate of the child's rate of development was made simultaneously with the measurement of the variables in adult speech, so it is not clear if it is the adults who influence the children or vice versa. Furthermore, in all the studies so far considered, the subjects were drawn from a restricted range of social background (predominantly middle class) and recorded in settings that were to some extent rendered atypical by the presence of the investigator. It must be concluded, therefore, that the extent to which fine-tuning is a general characteristic of adult speech to children is still uncertain, as is the nature of the relationship between such fine-tuning, if it occurs, and the course and rate of the child's linguistic development. The present study was carried out in an attempt to clarify some of these issues.

Design of the Study

The subjects were drawn from the 64 children in the younger cohort of the Bristol longitudinal study of language development, each of whom had been recorded at three-monthly intervals between the ages of 15 and 42 months. Three groups of children were selected who showed differing rates of development, as defined by the amount of time that elapsed between the recordings by which they had reached a mean length of utterance (MLU) of, first, 1.5 and, secondly, 3.5 morphemes. The Early Fast Developers (EFD) made this gain of 2 morphemes within six months and were all aged either 18 or 21 months when they reached the first developmental point. The Late Fast Developers (LFD) progressed at the same rate, but were on average six months older (i.e. 24 or 27 months) at the first developmental point. The Slow Developers (SD) all took 12 months or longer to register a 2 morpheme increase, and in fact five of the children failed to make this gain by the time of the last recording at 42 months. There were ten children in the SD group and eight in each of the others.

All recordings were made by means of a radio-microphone worn by the child, which picked up all speech by the child and all speech clearly audible to him or her. On each occasion, twenty-four 90-second samples were recorded at approximately 20-minute intervals between 9 a.m. and 6 p.m., the precise times, which were unknown to the subjects of the investigation, being determined by a pre-set automatic mechanism. From these 24 samples, 18 were subsequently drawn at random for transcription and coding. No observer was present during the recording, but the tape was played back to the parents in the evening and they were asked to recall, in as much detail as possible, the context, participants and content of each of the recorded samples of conversation. The speech data were thus drawn from a wide and naturally occurring range of contexts in and around the children's homes.

Following transcription and independent checking, each child utterance was coded according to a comprehensive scheme of linguistic analysis (Wells, 1975c), yielding a variety of developmental indices, four of which have been selected for the purposes of this study (see below). As adult utterances were given only a summary coding in the original study, the coding frame for adult speech, which is described below, had to be developed and applied specifically for this investigation.

Measures of Child Speech

Four indices of the child's level of language development were calculated at each developmental point:

(i) MEAN LENGTH OF STRUCTURED UTTERANCES (MLUS). This measure was calculated using the rules set out in Brown (1973), except that grammatically unstructured one-word utterances such as 'Yes', 'Please', 'Hello', etc., and idiomatic utterances such as 'All right', 'Here-you-are', etc., were omitted. (A justification for the use of this measure is given in Wells (1978a), where a number of alternative indices of development are discussed.)

(ii) RANGE OF MEANING RELATIONS ENCODED (SEMANTIC RANGE). This measure is based on a classification of the meaning relations expressed in the simple clause, organized in terms of the case configurations identified in the case grammar of Fillmore (1968) and Chafe (1970), e.g. categories such as agent, object, location. The classification is based on a two-dimensional matrix, in which one dimension is concerned with the basic state (e.g. physical attribution) or relationship (e.g. location in space) into which an entity may enter, and the other dimension is concerned with the static or changing nature of the state or relationship and, if changing, whether the cause of the change is specified (*cf*. Wells (1985a) for further details). Since the meaning relations so defined have been found to emerge in an order which is relatively constant across children, the number of different meaning relations encoded by a particular child can be taken as a good general indicator of his level of semantic development.

(iii) NUMBER OF MEANINGS EXPRESSED BY AUXILIARY VERBS (AUX. MEANINGS). The auxiliary verb system is an example of one of the systems specific to English which Newport *et al*. (*op. cit.*) considered might be susceptible to the influence of the mother's speech. This measure was calculated by counting the total number of meanings expressed through auxiliary verbs by each child. It was based on a description of the auxiliary verb by Wells (1979), in which 41 different meanings were recognized in the corpus collected from the 64 younger children.

(iv) COMPREHENSION. Given Cross's (1977) findings that parents responded most sensitively to the children's receptive abilities, we considered it essential to include a measure of comprehension. This took the form of the child's score on a language comprehension test which had 63 items of increasing difficulty, to which the child responded by acting out the meanings represented. As this test was administered at six-monthly intervals there was not always an administration of the test contemporaneous with an observation of spontaneous speech. In such cases the average of the scores from the preceding and following tests was used.

Measures of Adult Speech

The adult speech was coded in terms of 34 different speech

Enabling Factors in Adult-Child Discourse 47

variables, which were chosen to incorporate features of adult speech which previous studies had investigated (e.g. Cross (1977), Newport *et al.* (1977)) and also the different aspects, both communicative and formal, of adult-child discourse. In particular, categories were included which would enable us to focus on any variation in the weighting which individual adults might give to different interpersonal functions in their conversations. The variables investigated fall into four groups:

(i) LENGTH AND FORMAL COMPLEXITY. A number of variables concerned general features of adult-child discourse such as the proportion of adult utterances in relation to the total number of utterances produced by adult and child together; the average length of conversational sequences; and the proportion of sequences that were initiated by the adult rather than by the child. Further variables covered formal characteristics of adult speech, such as the mean length of utterances (MLUS), maximum utterance length (MLUL) and the difference between adult and child MLUS; also the proportion of utterances which constituted well-formed sentences and the number of verbs per utterance.

(ii) CONTEXT. The contexts in which sequences occurred were grouped into four mutually exclusive classes: household business; play with adult participation; general talk not related to household routine or play activities; watching TV and looking at books.

(iii) DISCOURSE FEATURES. The majority of adult speech variables measured a range of features of discourse, either the illocutionary functions of the adult utterances (statement; explanation; commissive, i.e. an utterance where the adult gives the child a choice to accept or refuse by means of an offer, suggestion, etc.; prohibition; instruction, either direct or indirect command; acknowledgement; request for clarification, confirmation; correction) or the various conversational devices used by adults to ensure topic incorporation and conversational continuity (repetitions and imitations; paraphrases; expansions and extensions; real and tutorial questions).

(iv) LOCUS OF REFERENCE. The final group of variables related to the referential features of the adult utterances, with each adult utterance coded according to whether the locus of reference was immediately present or displaced in time and, if the former, whether the activity involved the child alone, the adult alone or both together.

Analysis and Discussion of Results

Evidence Regarding the Extent of Fine-tuning

If adult speech to young children is finely tuned to the children's level of development, a comparison of adult utterances to the same children at two quite widely separated points in their development should show differences on at least some of the parameters investigated. Failure to find substantial stage-related differences would suggest that, although adults adopt an identifiable register when speaking to children, their speech is not finely adjusted to the level of communicative ability of the particular children with whom they are interacting.

In order to investigate the extent of adjustment in adult speech the scores on the adult language variables were first compared at the two measurement points.* Not surprisingly, substantial differences were observed in both average and maximum utterance length, with the adults producing longer utterances at the later measurement point. There was also a tendency for the average number of verbs per utterance to increase from the first occasion to the second. When the contexts in which adult speech was addressed to the children were compared, changes were found in the proportions occurring in different contexts. Whilst there was no substantial change in the proportion of speech occurring in contexts of Household Business, there was a significant decrease between the two occasions in the proportion occurring during Play and an increase in the proportion occurring in the context of General talk. There was also a trend towards an increase in the proportion occurring in the context of looking at books and watching television.

When the frequencies of particular discourse features were compared, the results were quite variable. There was no clear trend towards increase or decrease in the number of Acknowledgements, Instructions or Prohibitions. The number of Statements, on the other hand, showed a significant increase from the first to the second occasion, as did the number of Explanations. Conversational devices such as Expansions, Extensions, Imitations and Repetitions showed a tendency to decrease, although not significantly so, whilst the number of Corrections of various kinds increased significantly.

With respect to the locus of reference of adult utterances, the only significant change between the two observations was an increase in the number of utterances referring to objects and

---

*Results reported as significant are of the order $p \leq .05$; where a trend or tendency is reported, the value of p is greater than .05.

events outside the immediate situation.

Taking all these results together, there is clearly evidence of some degree of adjustment on the part of the adults as their children become more able to communicate linguistically. However, there is also evidence to suggest that, in many respects, adults continue to talk to children in very much the same way throughout the period delimited by the two observations. Before discussing these results further, however, we will present the results of a second method of analysis.

The second approach investigated the question of fine-tuned adjustment in adult speech by means of correlational analysis of the pooled data from both observations. Following Cross (1977), we considered that a substantial correlation coefficient between a variable in adult speech and an index of the level of the child's linguistic development would be evidence of fine-tuning in adult speech with respect to the variable concerned. The difference between this and the first approach is that in this case variance within observations as well as that between observations is included in the analysis, although the former must be limited in extent given the nature of the design of the study, which attempted to secure developmental equivalence in the children at each observation. In addition, four different measures of the child's level of linguistic development were included in the analysis.

Generally speaking, the results provide a strong confirmation of those obtained by the first approach. Both measures of utterance length in adult speech were positively associated with all child developmental indices, particularly with child MLU and Semantic Range, whilst decrease in the Difference between Child and Adult MLU was also significantly associated with all developmental indices. Average number of verbs in adult utterances increased with child MLU as did the proportion of adult utterances that were grammatically complete. There was a significant positive association between amount of speech in contexts of General Talk and all measures of child production, and a corresponding, though less significant, decrease in the context of Play, with the proportion in other contexts failing to show a significant change in relation to the child's increasing maturity.

The frequency of some discourse categories was found to be related to change in child speech; increase in Semantic Range in the child's speech correlated significantly with the frequency of Statements, Explanations and Corrections. At the same time the frequency of Expansions and Extensions was inversely related to the child's MLU. Reference to non-immediate events was also significantly related to the child's MLU and to his or her Semantic Range.

The correlations between the adult variables and all four child language indices indicate that where there was a significant association between a variable in adult speech and increase in the children's linguistic maturity, the strongest association tended to be with indices derived from spontaneous speech production and, amongst these, with Semantic Range. Correlations with child Comprehension were in all cases smaller and often not statistically significant.

This latter finding may be a reflection of the reduced sensitivity of the measure of comprehension for the reasons already mentioned, but the generally low level of correlation between adult speech variables and child comprehension must cast some doubt on the suggestion that adult speech is finely tuned to the child's concurrent level of comprehension, at least when this is measured independently of the interaction from which the adult measures are obtained.

Although both these analytic approaches show that a number of adult speech variables do show adjustment to the child's level of linguistic development, these represent quite a small proportion of the total number of variables investigated. This suggests that the extent of the 'fine-tuning' in adult speech adjustment, both within and between occasions, is not as great as had previously been supposed. Two possible explanations for this finding will be suggested. First, many of the variables investigated involve functions of language which have a continuing appropriateness throughout the period studied. Questions, for example, have important pragmatic and discourse functions in almost all kinds of spontaneous conversation, though the relative emphasis on securing new information as opposed to eliciting a contribution from a discourse participant in order to ensure conversational flow may well change from one situation to another and also with the level of ability to provide and encode new information on the part of the child (Halliday, 1975). The continuing high frequency of adult utterances which make reference to the activity of the child can also be seen as appropriate for the period under consideration. A substantial drop in the number of such utterances would, in fact, probably be a sign of poor adjustment on the part of the adult. For adult speech to be described as well adjusted to the child's developing ability, therefore, it may not be necessary to show changes on variables such as these.

An alternative explanation would be that the finely-tuned adjustments that were found in Cross's (1977) study of rapidly developing children are not characteristic of adults in general. Although there is strong evidence that the majority of adults do make adjustments in the length and complexity of their utterances, there is less evidence of a similar progressive adjustment in the functions for which adults speak. However, whilst fine-tuning on these variables does not seem to be characteristic of the majority of adults, it remains a possibility that it is a characteristic of the parents of rapidly developing children. If this is so, it would be plausible to suggest that such fine-tuning is actually facilitative of accelerated development. It is to this question that we now turn.

The Facilitative Effect of Adult Speech on Rate of Development

As the children in this study were selected to be equivalent in level of linguistic maturity at both developmental points, differing only in their rate of development, it is possible, by comparing the adult speech addressed to the three groups of children at the first developmental point, to discover which features of adult speech are associated with accelerated language development, and which are thus possibly facilitative of that development. To establish whether there were any between-group differences, the number of children in each group receiving speech which scored above or below the median score for the sample as a whole was compared on each adult speech variable.

No significant group differences for either utterance length or syntactic complexity were observed. There were also no major differences involving utterance context, although there was a slight trend for the adults with fast developing children (EFD) to engage in a higher proportion of conversations related to household business than adults with slow developing children (SD). There was also a trend for the EFD adults to produce more utterances per 27 minutes of conversation than the SD adults. However, the differential nature of the linguistic environment provided by the three groups of adults was most marked in the categories relating to discourse features and locus of reference. In each case, whenever there was a difference, the EFD adults produced substantially more exemplars than the SD adults while the LFD adults took up an intermediate position. Thus, those children who showed an early period of rapid language growth received significantly more Acknowledgements, Corrections, Prohibitions and Instructions than did those children who took 12 months or longer for an equivalent developmental growth. The EFD adults also produced substantially more Imitations and Repetitions, Total Questions, Indirect Commands and also more Direct Commands. In addition, more EFD adult utterances referred to Immediate Activity involving the Child Alone. Although the LFD group were in all cases intermediate between the EFD and the SD groups, no comparison between LFD and either EFD or SD groups achieved significance. Thus of the 34 parameters of adult speech coded in this study, the ten on which the EFD and SD adults can be clearly distinguished relate to discourse functions and locus of reference; there is no evidence of any clear distinction in either the utterance length or complexity of EFD and SD adult speech. Given that absolute frequencies rather than proportions of adult utterances were recorded on all those measures found to be significant and given also that there was a trend for EFD adults to produce more speech overall than SD adults, it would appear that quantity of speech may play an important part in accounting for rapid language development. We believe, however, that a case can be made for the importance of qualitative aspects of adult speech as well.

Acknowledgements, together with imitations and repetitions, which are often the stylistic realization of acknowledgements, probably have a supportive role but also help to provide children with the essential feedback which they require to verify the adequacy of their communicative efforts. A child who benefits frequently from expressed approval or evaluation is likely to discover more rapidly what relationships in the real world are salient and also to feel securer in his or her attempts to express them. Corrections probably operate in a similar way to acknowledgements, serving as another means of providing valuable feedback about the validity or appropriateness of the child's propositions. Corrections, however, were far less frequent in the data than acknowledgements.

Whereas both acknowledgements and corrections constitute adult *responses,* direct and indirect commands represent *initiating* utterances. There are a number of reasons why directives, both preventive and organizational, may be more facilitative for children with limited linguistic ability than other types of utterances, such as those serving a representational function. First, directive utterances occur frequently in the imperative form, which, because it is morphosyntactically simple, may be ideally suited to the child's limited processing capacity. Secondly, children at this stage may be specially suited to respond to directives. Shatz (1978) has demonstrated how children adopt an 'action responding' strategy, which treats any adult initiation as a directive unless there is substantial evidence to suggest otherwise. Thirdly, directives can be considered facilitative in that they are likely to encode semantic relations concerning objects and events with which the child is directly involved at the time of speaking. Parental commands may strongly aid development of the system of symbolic representation by encoding just those relations to which children are attending and which they have already represented to themselves enactively and/or iconically.

The tendency of parents to relate their speech with young children to contemporaneous events and objects has frequently been noted in previous studies (e.g. Messner, 1978; Ratner and Bruner, 1978). This study reports a clear relationship between amount of adult speech commenting on the activity in which the child alone is engaged and accelerated language development. This, together with the trend for EFD conversations to take place in the context of household business, suggests that those children whose language develops both early and rapidly are supplied with abundant language related to the routine household activities in which so much of the day is spent and to 'the ritualised encounters of child caring' which Ferrier (1978) considered likely to promote development in the early stages.

A further comparison of the adult speech to the three groups of children was made at the second developmental point. However, although suggestive of which features of adult speech may be facilitative at this later stage, the results cannot be taken as firm evidence, as we have no data on the children's rate of development after the 3.5 morpheme stage.

At the second point fewer significant differences were noted. Moreover, the pattern was no longer solely one of a strong contrast between EFD and SD adult speech, as there were also some clear differences between the speech of EFD and LFD adults and also between LFD and SD adults. At this later stage there is some evidence of the syntactic adjustments of the EFD adults being more finely tuned than those of the SD, for example the difference between the child's and the adult's MLU was notably larger for the SD than for the EFD. This, of course, may be a response to the differing ages of the two groups of children, the EFD adults matching their utterance length more closely to that of their children as a response to their younger age. Although there is again a definite trend for the EFD adults to produce more speech, the only discourse functions on which the difference between EFD and SD was significant were Statements and Commissives, with the EFD adults producing more in each case. EFD caretakers also produced substantially more utterances referring both to child only and to adults only activity, a result which may again reflect a response to the differences in the children's ages.

In general the LFD again assumed an intermediate position on most of the adult variables, but at the second point significant differences were observed between the number of Instructions produced by EFD and LFD, with the latter providing fewer, and also between LFD and SD adults with regard to child only references, where the LFD, like the EFD, produced more.

Clearly, those children who enjoyed a quantitatively rich verbal environment at the earlier point continue to do so as they become more linguistically mature, but the pattern of qualitative differences has shifted somewhat from that observed at the first developmental point. At the later point, those adults whose children had demonstrated accelerated language growth differ from those adults whose children had shown themselves slow developers with regard to the number of statements produced rather than in terms of acknowledgements or directives. This probably reflects the fact that the EFD adults are now responding to their children's increased capacity to process utterances other than those which can be dealt with by an 'action strategy'. The difference observed for commissives may reflect a greater preparedness on the part of EFD adults to confer authority for decision making on the children, now that they are older. We do not know, however, to what extent these differences relate to the subsequent rate of language development of the children in each group.

Summary and Conclusion

In order to establish the extent and nature of the adjustments in the speech adults address to their children and also to investigate whether differences in the ways adults talk to children can help to account for differences in the rate of the children's language development, the conversations of 26 children were coded in terms of a number of child and adult language variables which were then submitted to a number of analyses. The evidence regarding the existence of fine-tuning on the part of the adults was mixed; adjustments from one stage of language development to another occurred noticeably in utterance length and in syntactic complexity, less noticeably in conversational context and locus of reference and hardly at all in the various measures relating to discourse function. In contrast, there was strong evidence that differences in the frequencies of certain discourse functions, in particular acknowledgements, directives and questions, correlate with the differential rate at which the children mature linguistically, whereas no group differences relating to rate of development were observed for either utterance length or syntactic complexity.

In general, therefore, the results concerning adult speech adjustments do not fully corroborate Cross's (1977) fine-tuning hypothesis. We suggested that this might be either because it is not realistic to expect stage-related adjustments in such discourse functions as acknowledgements, commands and questions, or that fine-tuning may not be a characteristic of adults' speech in general. Cross's findings may in part reflect the fact that her subjects were middle-class mothers with rapidly developing children and also that her data were collected in an experimental setting which artificially stimulated the mothers to a higher level of speech-tuning than is normal in home contexts. The results of the present study, which utilized a more representative sample of adults and collected more naturalistic samples of speech, suggest that fine-tuning may not be a universal characteristic of adult–child conversation. The principal adjustments observed for the sample as a whole tend to be 'low-level' (Ervin-Tripp, 1978) (i.e. syntactic rather than related to conversational purpose) and there was some evidence to suggest that they may be related to the child's age instead of, or in addition to, the linguistic sophistication of the child.

The results obtained from the analysis of the adults' speech addressed to the three groups of children at the first developmental point confirm this view. Whereas all adults seem to monitor the syntactic level of their speech, those adults whose children showed accelerated language growth provide a language environment which is substantially different both in overall quantity of speech and in specific conversational purposes as compared with those adults whose children's language developed much more slowly. No group differences in either utterance length or syntactic complexity appeared. Thus, although speech adjustment is not substantial for the majority of adults, it may be finely tuned by those whose children develop rapidly. Moreover, the fact that those adults whose children showed a rapid but late-starting language growth appear to fall into an intermediate position on all those measures where significant differences were observed between the other two groups, suggests that, in the population as a whole, the level of adult speech adjustment relating to communicative intent may constitute a continuum with, at one pole, a group of adults highly sensitized to the communicative needs of their children and, at the other, a group of adults who monitor their speech only in coarse syntactic terms. This picture is something of an oversimplification but, to illustrate just how extreme the two poles can be, Table 1 compares the adult speech addressed, over an equivalent period of time at the first developmental point, to two children selected from the EFD and SD groups.

What this kind of evidence shows is that children whose language development is accelerated have provided for them a linguistic environment which is both quantitatively and qualitatively different from that experienced by slow developers. But does this allow us to conclude that such an environment is enabling?

Table 1: A comparison of the adult speech addressed to two children, one EED and the other SD, at the first development point

	Jonathan (EFD)	Maria (SD)
Adult MLU	4.17	4.11
Total questions	21	4
Instructions	50	16
Prohibitions	25	0
Direct commands	53	12
Indirect commands	11	0
Acknowledgements	42	6
Corrections	2	0
Imitations and repetitions	48	11
Child's age (in months)	21	21

Lieven's (1978) investigation of different patterns of verbal interaction in two mother–child dyads led her to conclude that it was the child who influenced the adult and not vice versa. Similarly, in the present study it is conceivable that the differential nature of the linguistic environment provided by the adult caretakers of the EFD and SD children was elicited by differences in linguistic ability between the two groups of children which the MLU measure on which they were equated failed to reveal. However, as no significant group differences on any of the other three child language variables could be detected, we consider such an interpretation unlikely. But this does not entirely rule out the possibility that adult speech differences occur as a response to differences in the children.

Although equivalent in terms of linguistic ability, the children may vary on a number of non-linguistic dimensions, such as personal interest, sociability, willingness to talk or ability to concentrate, any one of which may interfere with the establishment of an effective partnership with an adult. Before this issue can be satisfactorily resolved, therefore, we need to know far more about how these aspects of personality interrelate with the processes of language development.

However, irrespective of whether the observed differences in adult speech are elicited by differences between the children or are the result of differing adult strategies of interaction, or both, we believe that they represent a significant variation in the extent to which the children's linguistic environment facilitates their language development. Acknowledgements and corrections have a supportive function and provide the child with valuable feedback, while commands, particularly direct commands, may be ideally suited to the child's language processing abilities and communicative strategies at this early stage. In contrast, an enabling environment is not to be distinguished by the frequency of representational utterances as a whole, bearing out Halliday's (1975) observation that the representational model of language may be relatively late to emerge as important to the child.

Brown (1977) emphasized the importance of seeking to communicate with young children in order to facilitate their language development. We would agree with this advice and hope that we have been able to identify which particular aspects of communication may be especially facilitative at different stages of development. Although more work needs to be undertaken before it will be possible seriously to address the implications for intervention, it is to be hoped that, as the nature of adult–child communication slowly becomes clearer, the basis will be provided both for an understanding of why, despite the same linguistic competence, some children seem to become much more able language performers than others, and also for the construction of remedial language programmes. It is also evident that it will be necessary to take into account the child's stage of language development when deciding what particular features of verbal interaction to compensate for.

CHAPTER 4
Language and Learning: an Interactional Perspective

Introduction: Opposing Views of Language and its Acquisition

If one question more than any other has preoccupied students of language during the last 25 years it is 'where does language come from?' Clearly, language is learned, for each child grows up to speak the language of his or her surrounding community. But who has the greater responsibility for what is learned and the order in which learning takes place: the child or the people in his or her environment? Although the controversy goes back to classical times and perhaps even further, it was given new vitality in recent years by Skinner's (1957) behaviourist account of language learning and by Chomsky's (1959) innatist response. It was they who fired the opening shots, but the battle still continues today and neither side has yet won a clear victory.

One of the main reasons that the debate has continued so vigorously is that two quite different conceptions of language are involved: on the one hand, language as system and, on the other, language as resource (Halliday, 1978). For Chomsky and those who follow him, the central and most essential characteristic of language is its grammar – the finite system of implicitly known rules that enables a speaker or hearer to produce and understand a potentially infinite number of different sentences. To learn a language on this account is to construct a grammar – a set of complex and abstract rules, which relate meanings to sounds. Since these rules are not made available to the child either through inspection of other people's utterances or through direct instruction, the learning of them is seen as inexplicable except in terms of innately-given knowledge of the general principles underlying all human languages and a predisposition actively to construct and test hypotheses about the organization of the particular language to which the child is exposed.

However, what is missing from this first account, as those who argue for the importance of the environment point out, is any recognition of the pragmatic dimension of language – the uses to which it is put. When people interact with each other through language, the production of grammatically well-formed sentences is not an end in itself, but a means for acting in the world in order to establish relationships with others, to communicate information and to engage with them in joint activities. Children are thus born into a community of language *users* and their learning of language forms part of their socialization as members of that community. Acquiring control of the complex patterns of their native language is, therefore, on this second account, a matter of learning how to do things with language – 'learning how to mean,' as Halliday (1975) puts it. Through interacting with those in their environment, children thus both acquire the resources of the language of their community and learn how to make use of those resources in order to achieve a variety of purposes in relation to different people in different situations.

Both these accounts of language acquisition recognize that children must be equipped with the ability to learn a human language (in contrast to other species, which do not seem able to do so). Both also recognize that they will only learn if they grow up in a language-using environment. Where they differ is in whether they attribute the main responsibility for what is learned to the child or to the environment. In Chomsky's (1976) view, all that is required of the environment is the provision of instances of language in use in order to trigger the innate language acquisition device (LAD). To him, the fact that all normally functioning human beings learn their native language, despite wide differences in the nature of the 'primary linguistic data' to which they are exposed, makes it clear that the input plays little part in determining the particular course that development will take. In contrast, those who stress language as resource emphasize the interactional context in which language is learned and point to the wide variation between individuals in the degree of skill that is eventually acquired. Because language is concerned with the communication of meanings, they argue, it is essentially collaborative in nature. It is inconceivable, therefore, that children's experience of linguistic interaction should not have some influence on their learning. How important then, is the environment, or more specifically the experience of linguistic interaction with people in that environment, in determining what the child learns and the rate at which learning takes place? Since the answer to this question has far-reaching implications for the way in which we think about language and learning in school, the major part of this chapter will attempt an evaluation of the evidence bearing upon this issue which has emerged during the last quarter of a century.

The Evidence from Research

The Precursors of Language

From a strictly linguistic point of view, the learning of language does not begin until the child starts to produce recognizable words with the deliberate intention to communicate particular meanings. However, this ability does not emerge fully-formed from nowhere. Rather it is just one step in a developmental progression that starts much earlier and continues well on into adolescence. 'Cracking the code' may be the most difficult part of the total process, but before the child can embark on that task he or she first has to discover that there is a code to be cracked. How this happens is now beginning to emerge from studies of infants in the earliest weeks of life (*cf.* Lock, 1978). From the work of Trevarthen (1979) and Stern (1977), who observed and recorded infants interacting with their mothers, it appears that, long before they are able to interact with the physical world, infants are already behaving in ways that elicit responses from their parents and are thereby gaining feedback concerning the effects of their own behaviour. What both researchers noticed was that it is the infant who typically initiates the interaction and decides when it should end. However, it is the mother who, by the timing and aptness of her responses, gives continuity to the interaction in such a way that it looks as if the pair are engaging in something very like a conversation without words.

Initially, of course, it is most unlikely that the infant's gestures or vocalizations are intended to communicate. Nevertheless, as Newson (1978) puts it:

> Whenever he is is the presence of another human being, the actions of a baby are not just being automatically reflected back to him in terms of their physical consequences. Instead, they are being processed through a subjective filter of human interpretation, according to which some, *but only some,* of his actions are judged to have coherence and relevance in human terms . . . It is thus only because mothers impute meaning to 'behaviours' elicited from infants that these eventually do come to constitute meaningful actions so far as the child himself is concerned (p.37).

In other words, infants come to be able to have and express communicative intentions by being treated as if they already had them. These early interactions are almost exclusively social – establishing the interpersonal relationship between 'I' and 'You',

Language and Learning: an Interactional Perspective 61

addresser and addressee, which forms the basis of communication. But, towards the middle of the first year, they begin to incorporate objects and events in the world that mother and infant share and, in this way, the 'It' is added and the triangle of communication is completed. This may happen in a number of ways; through the adult following the infant's line of regard and giving him the object he appears to be interested in; by drawing the infant's attention to potentially interesting objects or events; or by marking through gesture and speech the steps in familiar sequences of activity such as feeding, bathing, dressing, etc. What is important about these early experiences, it is suggested, is that, although the infants have no language yet themselves, these interactional episodes provide a framework within which they can discover some of the fundamental principles upon which language in use is based – the reciprocal exchange of signals, the sequential patterning of turns, and the assumption of intentionality. Since adult speech, often ritually repetitive in form, accompanies the focal points in many of these transactions (Bruner, 1975; Ferrier, 1978), it seems reasonable to suppose that, by the later part of the first year, the child will also have formed a general hypothesis about the communicative significance of speech.

First Words

Treating speech as significant, however, is not the same thing as recognizing it to be meaningful. Perception of meaning entails the recognition that arbitrary but conventional patterns of sounds are intended, by virtue of that patterning, to bring about particular responses in the listener to aspects of the world that are shared with the speaker. To achieve this level of practical understanding, the child has to be able to:

(a) analyse the situation in order to form hypotheses about the meaning intention that the speaker is expressing;
(b) analyse the stream of speech sounds in order to segment it into units and discover the relationships between them;
(c) construct hypotheses about the way in which meanings and sounds are related to each other.

Stated in this form the task seems formidably difficult. In considering how the child sets about it, therefore, it may be helpful to consider the strategies that archaeologists might use in attempting to decipher an inscription in an unknown language on an artefact that they have unearthed. Typically, they try to work out, from their reconstruction of the context in which the object was found, the probable intention in producing it and, from that, the probable 'content' of the message. Armed with hypotheses of this kind, they can then attempt to interpret any regularities of patterning they can discover in the written symbols. If they can find and decipher sufficient inscriptions of this kind, they may eventually be able to reconstruct the language in which the inscriptions were written. Note, however, that, in the early stages of such a task, the inferences are almost entirely from conjectured meaning to linguistic form. Without fairly rich hypotheses about the content of the inscription it will never be deciphered, however easy it may be to recognize repeated patterns in the symbols themselves.

The same seems to be true for young language learners. In order to crack the code, they must have some way of producing hypotheses about the meanings of utterances that are addressed to them. In considering the earlier stage of pre-verbal communication, we have already seen how the infant might form rather general hypotheses about the uses that language serves in interpersonal communication, and it does indeed seem to be this aspect of language that is first attended to. Of course, it is very difficult to know precisely what children understand at this early stage, but their own utterances give us some clues as to the sort of uses that they are aware of. Halliday (1975), for example, on the basis of a study of his own son's language development, suggests that by the second half of the first year a child has discovered that utterances may be used to communicate four very basic kinds of intention, which he characterizes as 'instrumental', 'regulatory', 'interactional' and 'personal'.

Most of the child's utterances that express these functions consist of a single word, sometimes based on an adult word, sometimes one of his or her own invention. In context, however, the child's parents or other caretakers can frequently infer the intention and so, if the child attempts to express such intentions, it seems reasonable to assume that similar generalized intentions are also attributed to the utterances of others.

Somewhat later, on Halliday's account, three further functions are added, the 'heuristic', 'imaginative' and 'informative', the last probably not emerging until after the child has begun to produce multi-word utterances.

Although children's early utterances suggest that it is this pragmatic or interpersonal dimension of meaning that is paramount for them (Bruner, 1975; Dore, 1975; Griffiths, 1979), quite early they begin to comprehend and produce utterances that also have a referential function (McShane, 1980). Here, once again, it seems as if they may receive considerable help from the adults who interact with them. The 'naming game' is one that probably all children play with their parents or other caretakers (Brown, 1958), either in relation to real objects or, in Western cultures, in relation to representations of objects in picture books, magazines or mail order catalogues. From his studies of this particular interactional 'format', Bruner (Ninio and Bruner, 1978) concludes that the game has a repetitive and ritual character which renders the relationship between word and object salient. Equally, however, it appears that children must personally arrive at a hypothesis that there is a simple one-to-one relationship between single words and simple concepts, for otherwise how could they learn new words on the basis of a single hearing, as Carey (1978) has shown that they can and frequently do?

Rosch (1977) suggests that, in organizing and storing our experience, we tend to operate with what she calls 'prototype' examples of concepts – that is to say, with particularly clear examples. It seems likely that young children also form prototypical concepts and that these usually map quite easily on to the words that adults choose to use when talking to them. Thus, for example, 'bird' is the word most commonly used by adults to refer to all the species that most children are likely to see, and children initially respond similarly to all particular birds as instances of the same prototypical category, referring to all of them by the same word, 'bird', or by their own version of this word.

To match words to meanings in comprehending adult utterances, however, the child must also be able to identify the boundaries of the words in question in the stream of speech in which they occur. To a certain extent, this task is made easier by the fact that, in naming objects, adults frequently produce the name in isolation. However, this will not explain how the child identifies other words, such as verbs, prepositions, etc., which occur in isolation much less frequently. One clue is provided by the kinds of words that children begin to produce themselves, both at the single word stage and when they begin to put words together. In some of their early work, Brown and his colleagues (Brown and Bellugi, 1964) remarked on the 'telegraphic' nature of early utterances, and suggested that the words used tended to be those that are stressed in normal speech. Children, therefore, may use word stress to help them segment the stream of speech. This point has been made again more recently by Wanner and Gleitman (1982), who point out that in stressed languages generally, it is the unstressed items that are omitted in early utterances. Stress alone cannot be sufficient, however. Although it may give global salience to particular words, it does not give unambiguous information about word boundaries (e.g. 'an/orange' or 'a/norange'). To determine precisely where boundaries occur, the child must also notice how words combine with other words in the context of larger structures (e.g. 'an orange', 'my orange', 'this orange', etc.). Weir's (1962) study of her child's pre-sleep monologues shows how some children systematically try out possible combinations of this kind in what looks very much like playful practice.

First Sentences

Many of the child's single-word utterances consist of words that seem to refer to objects in the environment and this, in combination with contrasts in intonation, gesture and voice quality, allows adults to interpret them in context as conveying pragmatic intentions of the kinds described by Halliday. However, if they were to remain limited to single-word utterances, children would have very restricted powers of communication for, central to language, is its capacity to express relationships, such as actor–action ('the boy ran'), object–location ('Mummy is in the kitchen'), experiencer–state experienced ('I'm hungry') and so on. These relational meanings are typically realized grammatically – by word order, suffix or inflection – and are therefore not as transparent as those meanings that are lexicalized in individual words. Furthermore, there is rarely a direct, one-to-one relationship between meaning and formal realization. It is thus much more difficult for adults to attempt to teach the meaning–form relationships ostensively, as they frequently do with the names of familiar objects.

At this stage, therefore, children are much more heavily dependent on their own ability to form hypotheses about meanings and the ways in which these are related to the sequential patterns of morphemes that they can identify in the stream of speech. Where might such hypotheses come from?

Quite early in the post-Chomsky period of interest in language development, Donaldson (1966) suggested that the answer might be found in the cognitive schemata that the child has by this stage already constructed about the organization of the physical and social environment. Since then, a number of other researchers have pursued this line of investigation, often using Piaget's account of cognitive development as a basis for examining the relational meanings expressed in early utterances (and therefore also assumed to be understood). Brown, for example, concluded from his analysis of his own and other researchers' data 'that the first sentences express the construction of reality which is the terminal achievement of sensori-motor intelligence' (1973, p.200) and Edwards (1973) and Wells (1974) reached similar conclusions. However, although children certainly require the cognitive schemata which have aready been acquired in order to construct hypotheses about the meanings that are expressed in the speech that they hear, this is not in itself sufficient. They still have to discover which of the possible cognitive schemata are actually encoded in the language being learned and how they are organized in relation to the grammar. In a recent article summarizing developmental studies across a wide variety of languages, Slobin (1981) suggests that the method used by the child is to pay attention to what, following Rosch, he calls 'prototypical situations' – situations, that is, that are particularly salient, such as the transitive situation of an agent causing a change in the state or location of an object (e.g. 'Daddy (agent) is painting (cause change of state) the door (object)'). Treating these as basic semantic categories, the child then looks for the 'canonical', or basic grammatical, forms in which they are encoded. Whether this or some other strategy is the one that is actually employed, it is clear that the major responsibility for carrying out the task of mapping meanings on to forms, must lie with the child. Since they cannot be taught, each child must reinvent them for himself (Lock, 1980). However, it is still possible that the conversational context may facilitate the task to some degree. And during the last 15 years or so there has been an increasing number of studies which have attempted to find out whether this is in fact the case.

Modifications in Adult Speech to Children

The first of these studies were designed to rebut Chomsky's (1964) characterization of the input as 'random and degenerate'. And they were remarkably successful. Snow (1977), reviewing studies by a number of researchers, showed that there is very considerable evidence that caretakers do generally adjust their speech when talking to young children and that they speak a recognizable register of baby-talk, or 'motherese' as it has been called by some, which is characterized by formal simplicity, fluent and clear delivery and high redundancy in context.

Such characteristics certainly seem likely to facilitate the learner's task, but only in a rather general way. If one wanted to argue for a more specific effect of the input it would be necessary to demonstrate that it was, in addition, 'finely tuned' to the learner's current knowledge and progressively modified to present the child with precisely the information that he or she needed in order to take the next step. To some extent, adults do seem to behave in this way. Newport *et al.* (1977), Furrow *et al* (1979) and Wells (1980) have all found that the frequency with which adults addressed utterances to their children of the polar interrogative type (in which the auxiliary verb occurs in first position) was associated with the rate at which the children learned the auxiliary verb system. Nevertheless, no other formal characteristics of adult utterances have consistently shown a similar association.

Evidence of a rather different kind, however, is provided by the Bristol Language Development study (Wells, 1985a). This shows a remarkably close fit between the frequency with which particular sentence meanings, pronouns and auxiliary verbs occurred in the speech addressed to children and the order in which the items in these three systems emerged in the children's own utterances. Furthermore, the frequencies with which many of these items occurred at successive observations showed a sharp increase in the period immediately preceding the children's first recorded use of them. At first sight, therefore, it might appear that the adult input had the effect of determining the order in which the items were learned.

Nevertheless such a conclusion would be unwarranted, I believe. In the first place, for a fourth system investigated, that of utterance functions, the order of emergence was not significantly associated with the rank order of frequency of items in the input. On the other hand, when the effect of *complexity* was investigated – that is to say, the relative difficulty of particular items in terms of the number of semantic and syntactic distinctions involved and the level of cognitive functioning presumed to be required to cope with them – *all* of the linguistic systems examined showed a very substantial correlation between relative *complexity* and order of emergence, with the highest correlation ($r_s = 0.95$) occurring in relation to the system of utterance functions.

Complexity of what has to be learned, therefore, seems to be the main determinant of the order in which children's learning occurs, rather than the relative frequency with which the items are used in the speech that is addressed to them. Secondly, since the order in which learning occurs is remarkably similar across children (Wells, 1985a), it would be necessary, if the main burden of explaining this order were to be placed on the frequency characteristics of the input, to attribute something like 'omniscience' to the adults who interacted with them (Shatz, 1982). For they would not only have to know, in some sense, the order in which future learning would occur, but also be able to time the frequency with which they used particular items to anticipate the sequence of development. Although it is possible that some adults are able to do this, it seems most unlikely that all adults would be able to do so. A more plausible explanation would seem to be that the order in which learning occurs results from an interaction between learners who are pre-adapted to learn in a particular way and the relative complexity of the items in the language to which they are exposed.

The fact that, for some linguistic systems at least, there is also a close match between order of learning and input frequency can best be explained in terms of responsive behaviour by adults. As already noted, adults tend to simplify their speech in order to be comprehended by their children. They therefore tend not to use items that they find their children cannot understand. However, when an occasional use of a more difficult item to a child is responded to with apparent comprehension, they begin to use that item more frequently. And, since children soon begin to produce items which they have assimilated through comprehension of the speech of others, the emergence of an item in their own speech follows shortly after an increase in the frequency with which it is addressed to them. Thus it is the cues provided by the child that lead to changes in adult behaviour rather than vice versa.

The Relative Contribution of Child and Environment

Having surveyed a selection of the evidence available in relation to the main stages of discovering and cracking the linguistic code, we are now in a position to try to evaluate the relative contributions of the child and of the environment to the achievement of this complex task. To help us in this endeavour it may be useful to recall the initial distinction made between language as system and language as resource.

Viewed from the perspective of language as system, it is difficult, as Chomsky and others have argued, to see how the environment can have anything more than an enabling function. Speech addressed to the child provides instances of language in use, but the forming and testing of hypotheses about the relationship between language and experience and about the internal organization of the language system itself can only be carried out by the learner. Clearly, if the input were to be seriously impoverished as, for example, if it contained no instances of declarative sentences, this would certainly impede or distort the child's construction of the language system. On the other hand, above a certain fairly minimal threshold, the relative frequencies of items in the input do not, in themselves, appear strongly to influence the sequence of learning.

Furthermore, since all but the most seriously handicapped children succeed in constructing their knowledge of their native language in an almost identical sequence, despite quite wide variation in the amount and quality of the input, it seems reasonable to suppose that the sequence of learning is very largely controlled by the innate structure of the learner's mind. What this structure is, however, and whether it is specific to language or more generally involved in cognitive processing, is still far from clear.

Pressure to succeed in communicating may go some way towards explaining the motivation for the self-activated learning that takes place (Bates and MacWhinney, 1982) but, beyond that, there seems to be a built-in determination to master the system for its own sake – to regard language as 'an internal problem space *per se*' (Deutsch, 1981). It is only such a conceptualization of the child as language learner that can account for the well-known phenomenon of over-regularizations (e.g. 'goed', 'mouses', etc.) and the sorts of errors in older children's speech which have been carefully documented by Bowerman (1982), or explain their imperviousness to adult attempts to correct their speech. Models provided by others are only of use when children have reached the stage of being able to assimilate them to their own developing systems.

However, if the role of the environment in relation to the learning of language as system is restricted to the provision of primary linguistic data, such a limitation is very far from being the case when one adopts the perspective of language as resource. It is only from interaction with other people in particular situations that children can discover the appropriate ways of deploying their resources to achieve particular intentions – or indeed discover the existence of the linguistic code in the first place. Furthermore, in all these aspects of learning to be a language user, the quality of the child's interactional experience has been found to be significantly related to the rate at which learning takes place.

In the very early pre-linguistic stages, for example, Ainsworth *et al.* (1974) showed that mothers with the greatest responsive sensitivity to their infants during the first months were the ones with the most linguistically advanced children at the end of the first year. At the stage of early vocabulary learning in the second year, too, Nelson (1973) found that rapid acquisition of the first 50 words was associated with a maternal style that was both accepting of the child's contributions and non-directive of the interaction.

By the end of the second year, when the child has already begun to construct a grammar, it is still the same sort of parental behaviour that is found to be associated with rapid progress. From the Bristol study (Barnes *et al*., 1983) comes evidence that such progress is associated with the frequency with which adults pick up and extend the meaning expressed in the child's previous utterance. Similarly, Cross (1978) found that a group of children selected because they were accelerated in their progress received a significantly greater number of sequences of adult speech which both expanded and extended their previous utterances than did a sample of children making normal progress. Even with some handicapped children, such as the deaf, it has been found that the same adult qualities of contingent responsiveness are the ones that most facilitate their linguistic development (Wood, in press).

What these findings all suggest, then, is that what is most important in the behaviour of children's parents and other caretakers is sensitivity to their current state – their level of communicative ability and their immediate interests – and to the meaning intentions they are endeavouring to communicate; also a desire to help and encourage them to participate in the interaction. To be a careful and sympathetic listener and to respond to the meaning intended by the speaker are qualities that characterize the behaviour of conversationalists of any age, if they are genuinely concerned to achieve mutual understanding; such qualities are particularly important when interacting with a much less adept conversational partner.

In the very early stages of the child's development as a conversationalist, it is inevitable that the adult must take the major responsibility for managing the interaction (Kaye and Charney, 1980) but as Bruner remarks in his discussion of the 'Language Assistance System' (LAS):

> The first thing to note about the adult role in this system is the adult's willingness to share or even hand over control to the child once he has learned to fulfil the conditions on speech. However obvious this may seem, it is a *sine qua non* of the adult's role in the system (1981, p.45).

Handing over control and being prepared to negotiate meanings and purposes are the characteristics that we have also noticed among facilitating adults in the Bristol data. The following example, in which 3½-year-old Jonathan is helping his mother by polishing his wardrobe demonstrates this.

J: Do you think this is lovely?
M: I think it's a bit smeary
J: Why do you think it's bit smeary?
M: Because you put far too much polish on
* * (inaudible)
M: Right,
Now you can put the things back on there (on the dresser)
And I'll put the carpet-sweeper over the room
J: Well why can't I put the carpet-sweeper over the room?
M: Because that's my job OK?
J: What is my job?
M: You've done your job
You've polished the furniture

[a little later]

J: It doesn't matter if that polish goes in your eyes does it?
M: Oh it does yes
It makes them sting
J: * (inaudible)
M: It makes them sting very badly
J: Well just now some of that polish waved in my eye
M: Did it?
J: Yes
M: Do they sting? (i.e. your eyes)
Or did it miss?
Don't rub them with the duster darling (v)
The duster's all dirty

J: Well how can that get out Mummy? (referring to polish)

```
                        M: Why don't you go and wipe
                           it with the flannel in the
                           bathroom
                                      [J goes to bathroom]
J: No I think I'll get it out with
   the towel
   Mummy I just have to see if I
   can get it out with this towel.
                        M: All right.
```

It would seem, therefore, that adults like Jonathan's mother are intuitively aware that the major responsibility for actually mastering the resource of language rests with the child rather than with themselves and that their role is essentially one of sustaining and encouraging the child's self-activated learning.

Language and Learning in Later Childhood

The emphasis so far has been on learning language rather than on learning through language. However, in practice, the two are to a very considerable extent co-extensive. Just as children learn the language system through experience of using it as a resource, so in increasing their control of the resources of language they also increase their understanding of the experiences that are encoded by those resources. The speech addressed to them not only provides evidence about the way in which the language system works but also about the world to which the system refers.

The significance of this parallelism is far-reaching for it implies that, in so far as the child's learning takes place through linguistic interaction with more mature members of his or her culture, the responsibility for what is learned should be shared between learner and teacher in the same kind of way that it was in the early stages of language acquisition: the child expressing an interest in some object or event and the adult sharing that interest and helping the child to take it further.

To a considerable extent this is what happens in the pre-school years at home, particularly for the children who make the most rapid progress. However, even in such homes, sustained discussion of a single topic is relatively rare and there is very little adult speech that looks like deliberate instruction. Most of the talk arises out of ongoing activity and takes on its significance from the purposes of those involved; at home, learning, like talking, is for the most part instrumental to the task in hand. As the example above shows, some of the richest opportunities for talking and learning occur when child and adult are engaged in collaborative activity, such as carrying out household tasks, like cooking or cleaning.

However, the most enriching experience of all for many children is probably the open-ended exploratory talk that arises from the reading of stories. Several investigators have noted how much more complex, semantically and syntactically, is the language that occurs in this context (Snow, 1977; Heath, 1983). It also has a particularly important contribution to make to the child's imaginative development (Meek, 1985). Furthermore, the frequency with which children are read to has been found to be a powerful predictor of later success at school (Wells, 1985b).

The learning that takes place on such occasions is of particular significance, for not only does the discussion provide an opportunity for children to relate the characters and events of the imaginary world to their own first-hand experience, but it also introduces them to the potential that language has, particularly in the written mode, to create alternative 'possible worlds' through words. As Donaldson (1978) emphasizes, in order to meet the demands of formal education, the child needs to learn to disembed his or her thinking from the context of immediate activity and to operate upon experience, both real and hypothetical, through the medium of words alone. Stories, and the talk that arises from them, provide an important introduction to this intellectually powerful function of language.

Observation of children in their homes, then, shows that, as with the initial learning of language, the motivation to learn *through* language comes from within, as they actively seek to gain control of their environment and to make sense of their experience. Once the child can use his or her linguistic resources to operate on that experience, though, the contribution of other people increases enormously in importance. For it is through the power of language to symbolize 'possible worlds' that have not yet been directly experienced, that parents and, later, teachers can enable children to encounter new knowledge and skills and to make them their own.

In school, where classes consist of 30 or more children, the task is not an easy one. A teacher has to ensure that all children acquire the skills of literacy and numeracy and extend their knowledge in the areas prescribed by the curriculum, whilst at the same time respecting the sense-making strategies that each child has already developed and recognizing the individuality of the internal model of the world that each child has already constructed and the interests he or she has developed. As in learning to talk, however, the child will be helped most effectively by teacher strategies of guidance and contingent responsiveness (Wood, 1983) – listening attentively in order to understand the child's meaning and then seeking to extend and develop it. This view of the teacher as essentially a facilitator of learning was strongly emphasized by Vygotsky, 50 years ago, in his discussion of the 'zone of proximal development'. As he put it, 'what the child can do today in cooperation, tomorrow he will be able to do alone' (trans. Sutton, 1977). The crucial word in that statement is 'cooperation'. A fuller understanding of the nature of linguistic interaction, whether at home or in the classroom, is leading us to recognize that, to be most effective, the relationship between teacher and learner must, at every stage of development, be collaborative. Teaching, thus seen, is not a didactic transmission of pre-formulated knowledge, but an attempt to negotiate shared meanings and understandings.

CHAPTER 5
Some Antecedents of Early Educational Attainment

During the late 1960s and early 1970s a great deal of attention was given to the subject of educational 'underachievement', particularly among lower-class children, and 'linguistic disadvantage' was often suggested as one of the principle causes. Whether the problem was conceived in terms of code orientation (Bernstein, 1971), range of uses of language (Tough, 1973), or dialect and perception of the social context (Labov, 1970), almost all researchers saw the disadvantage of the lower-class child as arising from an incompatibility between the (predominantly middle-class) linguistic demands and expectations of the school and the forms and uses of language learned in the different cultural settings of the family and the immediate neighbourhood, in the course of everyday, spontaneous conversation. However, very little systematic empirical evidence was advanced by any of these researchers to support their arguments and so the assumptions: (a) that there is linguistic incompatibility between home and school, greater in the case of lower-class children, and (b) that this incompatibility is a major contributory factor in educational underachievement, tended to be accepted on the basis of their plausibility rather than because they had been clearly demonstrated (Edwards, 1976).

One of the aims of the most recent phase of the Bristol Language Development Programme has been to test these assumptions by means of a longitudinal study, starting at the age of 15 months and continuing into the early years of schooling. The 32 children who form the subjects of this particular phase of the research were drawn from the sample of 128 children whose pre-school language was investigated in the first phase of the programme. The original stratified sample, consisting of two sub-groups aged 15 and 39 months respectively at the time of the first observation, was selected from an initial random sample drawn from the total pre-school population of Bristol of the appropriate ages. In stratifying the sample, equal representation

Some Antecedents of Early Educational Attainment

was given to both sexes, four divisions of the spectrum of family background and all four seasons of the year with respect to month of birth. The sub-sample for the present study was selected from the younger group in such a way as to maintain as closely as possible the representativeness of the original sample, whilst ensuring that they covered the full range of oral language ability as measured at the age of 3½ years (see below).

Ten observations, involving recordings of spontaneous conversation in their homes and the administration of tests in the University, had already been made of each of these children at three-monthly intervals between 15 and 42 months. These were supplemented in the present study by a further recording in the home just before each child started school and by three similar recordings in the children's classrooms during the first, second and sixth terms in school. In addition, tests were administered in the first and sixth terms at school, and the children were simultaneously assessed by their teachers. Interviews were also carried out with the parents when the children were approximately 3½, 5 and 7 years old.

Because the children's homes were widely dispersed throughout the city of Bristol, 27 different schools were involved, in the first instance, with the children's entry to school being spread over four school terms in 1976–1977. However, as a result of moves by the children and of changes in teaching staff, by the end of the study the number of schools involved had increased to 30 (one child moved too far from Bristol for the final observation to be made) and the number of teachers to more than 70. Thus, in spite of the small size of the sample, it includes families, teachers and LEA schools from the full range to be found in the city.

This chapter reports the results of a retrospective analysis of these longitudinal data in an attempt to determine the relative contributions of a variety of variables in predicting educational attainment at seven years of age.

The Data to be Analysed

The variables included in this investigation fall into five main groups:

1. Profiles of language ability and of adult speech addressed to the children in the early pre-school years, derived from the recordings of spontaneous conversation.
2. Children's scores on the various tests administered on entry to school and at the end of the sixth term.

3. Teachers' assessments of the children's academic skills and social behaviour on entry to school and at the end of the sixth term.
4. Responses from parental interviews concerning the children's home environment and the parents' preparation of the children for school and help with school work.
5. Scores derived from analyses of the home recording just prior to school entry and from the recordings of classroom interaction.

Each of these will be briefly described in the following paragraphs.

1a. Profiles of Language Ability

For each of the three monthly recordings, all child utterances were coded for a wide variety of linguistic variables (Wells, 1975c). From these, seven were selected as representing a profile of the child's level of productive linguistic ability: mean length of structured utterances (MLUS); mean length of five longest utterances; range of basic sentence meanings expressed; number of different types of semantic modification (e.g. time, aspect, modality, manner, etc.); number of different auxiliary verb meanings; syntactic complexity; range of functions that utterances were used to perform (Wells, 1978a,b). These were then converted to z scores and an aggregate score computed at two ages: 2 years and 3½ years.

1b. Parental Speech to Child

Following earlier studies by Cross (1977; 1978), Furrow et al. (1979) and Newport et al. (1977), the adult speech addressed to the children (mainly by their parents) when they had reached an MLU of 1.5 morphemes in their structured utterances was coded for a number of features of form, context, locus of references, discourse function and relationship of the adult's utterance to the preceding child utterance or current activity (Wells, 1980). A subsequent principal components analysis (Barnes et al., 1983) identified six major components, of which four were significantly associated with the children's rate of progress: absolute amount of adult speech; frequency of semantic extensions of the child's meaning; frequency of direct requests in the context of control of the child's behaviour; frequency of polar interrogatives. Scores on these variables were taken as indices of the facilitative quality of adult speech experienced by the child in the early stages of language development.

2. Tests

The tests administered on entry to school at five years were intended to provide an estimate, obtained under controlled conditions, of certain aspects of the children's readiness for the more formal type of education that they would meet at school. They included an 'acting-out' test of oral comprehension of a story involving a family at home (Wells and Raban, 1978); a question-and-answer test based on an orally presented story (Evans *et al.*, 1978); the English Picture Vocabulary Test (Brimer and Dunn, 1963); a test of Knowledge of Literacy (Wells and Raban, 1978) derived from the tests constructed by Clay (1972b); a visual and motor coordination test (Evans *et al.*, 1978), based on the work of Frostig (Frostig and Horne, 1973).

At the end of the sixth term, the EPVT was repeated and three further tests were administered: the Neale Analysis of Reading Ability – Accuracy and Comprehension (Neale, 1969); and a test of number operations (Wells and French, 1980).

Overall test scores were constructed at each age by aggregating z scores from each of the separate tests.

3. Teacher Assessments

Because tests can only sample a relatively narrow range of pupil's knowledge or ability and because we found that, compared with their middle-class peers, lower-class children tended to achieve lower scores on tests than on measures derived from spontaneous conversation (Wells, 1978b), we felt it important to obtain an assessment of each child based on the teacher's experience, over an extended period of time, of his or her behaviour in the naturally occurring situations of the classroom. A further reason for asking the teachers to make these assessments was to allow a comparison to be made between the evaluations of the children's abilities made by a group of professional educators and the results of the tests administered in the same classrooms but under controlled conditions.

Each assessment consisted of a number of sections covering: (i) social adjustment; (ii) language ability (oral language only in term one, oral and written language in term six); (iii) other academic abilities (number and 'matching' in term one, number and logical concepts in term six); and (iv) physical development. Items took the form of alternative behavioural descriptions, the most appropriate of which the teacher was asked to tick for the child concerned, e.g.

Ease of understanding oral language:

(a) understands instructions and questions without difficulty
(b) sometimes needs one or two repetitions before he/she understands
(c) needs to have almost everything repeated several times before he/she understands.

There were also a number of summary items, on which the teacher was asked to rate the child using a five-point scale centering on average. However, only the social, linguistic and other academic abilities sections were used in calculating aggregate scores for each assessment.

4. Parental Interviews

Two interviews were administered: one parent (usually the mother) was interviewed just prior to each child's entry to school, then both parents were interviewed at the end of the sixth term. In both cases, interview schedules were prepared with questions that called either for factual information or for opinions and evaluations that could be assigned to an interval on a predetermined scale. The two examples on p.79 illustrate the formats used.

Questions were read aloud, always in the same form, and the interviewer, having listened to the answer, marked the appropriate response category. In case of doubt, the interviewer would check with the respondents that he or she had correctly encoded their answer; parents were also invited to add any information that they thought was relevant, and this was recorded in note form where it amplified or qualified the coded response.

In the first interview, in addition to seeking information about the siblings, if any, and about changes in the parents' occupations or education since the earlier phase of the research, questions were asked; (i) about the child's pre-school experience and preferred activities; (ii) about the functions for which they had observed the child to use language; (iii) about any steps the parents had taken to prepare the child for school, with further probe questions where responses made specific reference to activities concerned with literacy; and (iv) about the parents' knowledge of, and attitudes to, the child's school and their own role in the child's education.

In the second interview, having repeated the questions about family background, further questions were asked: (i) about the parents' own uses of, and opinions about, literacy; and (ii) about their interests and involvement in the child's activities at school, with probe questions to elicit specific details if mention was made of helping the child with school work at home.

Question 6A (at age five)

Here are some things that – might enjoy doing. I'd like you to tell me how often you think – does these different activities.

On card to be handed to parent

Very often – at least once a day	1
Often – most days	2
Quite often – more than once a week	3
Sometimes – about once a week	4
Not very often – less than once a week	5

Helping you around the house
Playing make-believe games like 'mothers and fathers'
Riding a bike or playing on swings and slides
Writing or pretending to write
Playing with little toys, like dolls, cars or animals
Listening to a story being read aloud
Watching television
Playing with paints.   etc.   etc.

Are there any other favourite activities that happen very often that I haven't mentioned? . . . .

Question 10 (at age 5)

How does – feel about starting school would you say?

Is looking forward to it very much	1
Is quite looking forward to it	2
Has no feelings either way	3
Is not too happy about it	4
Is really not looking forward to it.	5

Two examples of question formats

5. *Recordings at Home and at School*

The quality of children's home and classroom experience of linguistic interaction – whom they interact with, what they do and how their activities are directed and evaluated in the two settings, together with the extent of the difference between them – seem likely to have an important influence on their school attainment and we are currently attempting to derive measures of this sort from the recordings of naturally-occurring conversation in the two settings. However, at the time of writing these analyses have not yet been completed and so results from them have not been included in the present chapter. (The results of a limited analysis of the last home recording will be discussed in the final section.)

Analyses and Results

With such a multi-faceted longitudinal study, the different kinds of data collected lend themselves to a variety of analyses, some of them of considerable interest in their own right. The recordings of spontaneously occurring conversation, for example, have already given rise to a number of investigations of interaction between children and their parents (Wells, 1980; Wells *et al.*, 1979; Barnes *et al.*, 1983) and between teachers and pupils (French and MacLure, 1980; MacLure and French, 1981; Wells and Montgomery, 1981). Here, however, space only permits consideration of the data in terms of a retrospective analysis of the antecedents of educational attainment at age seven years.

Two estimates of attainment at age seven were available: the aggregate score from the tests and that from the teacher assessment. The correlation between these two sets of scores was $r = .70$ ($p<.001$). Scores on each of the predictor variables were correlated with both these indices of attainment. The results are presented in Table 1.

Secondly, using the combined rank orders from both estimates of attainment, two groups each of nine children were identified as High and Low Attainers and the scores of these two groups on each of the predictor variables were compared, using the Mann-Whitney U Test, to determine whether differences between the scores of High and Low Attainers were statistically significant. The results are also presented in Table 1.

As might be anticipated, of all the independent variables, the two assessments of the children on entry to school are found to be the strongest predictors of attainment at seven years. Of the two, the tests are considerably more successful than the teacher

Table 1 Predictors of educational attainment at 7 years

Predictor Variables	Tests at 7 years r=	T. assess. at 7 years r=	High vs. Low z=
From Recordings			
Language profile at 2 years	.45*	.24	2.03*
Language profile at 3½ years	.49**	.31	1.86
Amount of adult talk	.49**	.30	1.90
MLU of adult speech	.04	.01	0.49
Number of adult polar interrogatives	.02	−.05	0.89
Number of adult direct requests in control (When Child MLU = 1.5 Morphemes)	.22	−.13	0.13
Number of adult imitations	.42*	.22	1.33
Number of adult extensions	.40*	.20	1.31
From Parental Interview Pre-School			
Amount of mother talk pre-speech	.51**	.42*	1.84
Mother working	−.02	−.12	0.34
Attendance at playgroup	.30	.37*	1.15
Attendance at nursery	−.26	−.28	1.13
Total playgroup/nursery attendance	.02	.03	0.14
Mother's time with child	.14	.29	0.60
Range of child activities	.44*	.59***	2.21*
Child interest in adult activities	.18	.26	0.20
Child interest in TV	.05	.24	0.30
Child interest in literacy	.49**	.63***	1.60
Child concentration in literacy	.69***	.66***	2.63**
Number of book owned by the child	.59***	.62***	2.18*
Child read/write by 5 years	.42*	.35	2.44*
Child talkativeness	.00	.01	0
Child range of language functions	.44*	.23	1.55
Parents' estimate of child lang. ability	.25	.42*	1.47
Parent-child talk about school	.32	.27	1.19
Parent expectations about school	.22	.21	0.90
Parent preference for informal education	.26	.18	1.40
Parents' interest in literacy	.45*	.53**	1.56

*p<.05   **p<.01   ***p<.001

Table 1 Predictors of educational attainment at 7 years, cont'd

Predictor Variables	Tests at 7 years r=	T. assess. at 7 years r=	High vs. Low z=
Tests on Entry to School			
Acting-out story comprehension	.61***	.61***	2.46*
Questions on story comprehension	.57***	.56***	2.78**
English Picture Vocabulary Test	.64***	.43*	2.13*
Knowledge of Literacy Test	.79***	.62***	3.49***
Visual and Motor Coordination Test	.62***	.33	1.90
Aggregate Test Score	.83***	.66***	3.05**
Teacher Assessment on Entry to School			
Social Development	.19	.27	0.31
Oral Language Ability	.64***	.44*	2.61**
Other Academic Abilities	.53**	.47**	2.39*
Aggregate Assessment Score	.51**	.46**	2.30*
Assessment of Accent and Dialect	.19	.22	0.31
From Parental Interview at 7 years			
Amount of parents' reading	.36*	.31	0.80
Parents' views on importance of literacy	.21	.17	0.14
Knowledge of child's activities at school	.45*	.38*	1.57
Parents' visits to school	.26	.33	0.14
Parents' views on own role in education	.24	.19	1.10
Amount of help given	.50**	.31	1.31
Satisfaction with child's progress	.18	.37*	1.30
Child's position in family	.46**	.33	3.19**
Class of family background	.58***	.51**	3.01**

*p<.05   **p<.01   ***p<.001

assessments in predicting later attainment, however estimated, and this is also generally true of the individual tests, although the EPVT and the test of visual and motor coordination are not as successful as the other tests in predicting the later teacher assessment. Of the various parts of the earlier teacher assessment, the section concerned with oral language ability gives the strongest predictions of later attainment. However, the strongest single predictor is the test of Knowledge of Literacy, with correlations of $r = .79$ and $r = .62$ with the later test and teacher assessment estimates of attainment respectively. Comparing the High and Low Attainers, similar results are observed, with the scores of the high attainers being significantly greater than those of the low attainers on all but one of the tests and on the teachers' assessments of oral language and other academic abilities.

Some of the responses from the second parental interview also predict attainment at seven, suggesting that the role of the parents during the first two years of schooling is not insignificant. Parents who themselves read more are likely to have more successful children ($r = .36$, $p<.05$; $r = .31$, n.s.)*; of greater importance, however, is the parents' knowledge of what their children are doing at school ($r = .45$, $p<.05$; $r = .38$, $p<.05$) and the amount of help that they give with school work ($r = .50$, $p<.01$; $r = .31$, n.s.). There is some difficulty in interpreting this latter result, however; several of the children with the highest attainment had, in their parents' opinions, made such rapid progress that, at the time of the interview, there was no need for the parents to give the sort of help that was specified in the categories coded. For example, the children no longer needed anybody to listen to them read or to help them with writing or number work, because they were already competent. Such parents often mentioned other types of help given, such as discussions of matters of general interest, looking at reference books or 'educational' visits, but these activities were not amongst those specifically coded. The scores for these children thus almost certainly underestimate the parental contribution and so reduce the size of the obtained correlations.

Responses to the questions in the first parental interview were generally concerned with the children as they were in the months immediately preceding entry to school: the range of their interests and activities, their use of language and the content of their interactions with their parents. Not all of these variables have been included in Table 1, but those that have been omitted are not significant as predictors of later attainment. It is interesting to note, however, that neither the amount of time that mother worked during the pre-school years nor attendance at play-group or nursery is associated with attainment at age seven. The trend

---

*In reporting correlation coefficients, the first figures in each case refer to the aggregate test scores and the second to the aggregate teacher assessment scores at seven years.

for nursery attendance to be associated with low attainment could perhaps be explained in terms of priority being given in nursery schools and classes to children already judged at age three to be educationally 'at risk'; however the correlations between amount of nursery school experience and the aggregate scores on tests and teacher assessment on entry to school, although negative ($r = -.26$ and $-.33$ respectively), are both non-significant. The correlation between nursery experience and the language profile at 3½ years ($r = -.20$) is also non-significant.

The variables from the interview that make positive predictions of later attainment concern the range of children's activities ($r = .44, p<.05; r = .59, p<.001$) and particularly their interests and activities in the area of literacy ($r = .49, p<.01; r = .63, p<.001$). The span of their concentration in such activities, in particular ($r = .69, p<.001; r = .66, p<.001$), is a very strong predictor of later attainment. As might be expected, therefore, there is also a significant association between the parents' concern to share their own interests in literacy with their children and the children's later attainment ($r = .45, p<.05; r = .53, p<.01$). These results are confirmed by the comparisons between High and Low Attainers: high attainers are significantly more likely than low attainers to take part in a wide range of activities, to possess a large number of their own books, to have acquired some minimal skills in reading and writing before starting school and to concentrate for extended periods on activities involving reading, looking at books, writing, scribbling and painting.

Going back still further to the evidence from the recordings of spontaneous interaction in the early stages of language development, it can be seen that later educational attainment is predicted by scores on the language profiles at both 2 and 3½ years and by the indices of the quantity and quality of the talk experienced with parents and other adults, although it is only with the aggregate test scores at seven years that the correlations are statistically significant. However the importance of adult speech from the very earliest stage is indicated by the significant correlations ($r = .51, p<.01; r = .42, p<.05$) between both the estimates of later attainment and the mothers' assessments of how much they talked to their children before the children could talk at all.

Finally, there are two variables which, although derived from the second parental interview, are descriptive of the children's social environment throughout most or all of the period under investigation. The first of these concerns the child's position in the family.

It has often been suggested that a child's position in the birth order affects his or her experience in ways which influence subsequent school attainment. However, whilst this is almost certainly true, it seems likely that it is not birth order as such which is important but rather such factors as the age-gaps involved, whether the particular child spends most of his or her time with an older or younger sibling, and how much undivided attention is received from parents, which is influenced as much by the number of pre-school age children in the family as by actual position in the birth order. In constructing the index of child's position in the family, therefore, scores were assigned as follows:

Only child or eldest child with no close siblings: 4
First born with one or more close siblings: 3
Subsequent born with no close siblings: 2
Subsequent born with one or more close siblings: 1
(Close = less than three years apart)

Measured in this way, it is found that a child's position in the family is a significant predictor of later attainment as measured by tests ($r = .46$, $p<.01$); it is also a variable on which High and Low Attainers are significantly distinguished ($z = 3.19$, $p<.001$).

Class of Family Background is still more of a summary variable. Used to stratify the population for the construction of the sample for the first phase of the research programme, its calculation took account of the occupational status and terminal level of education of both parents, with occupation being scored on a 5-point scale using the Registrar-General's categorization I–V, and education being categorized as either minimal (4 points) or more than minimal (2 points). This yielded a 13-point scale, which was then divided into four roughly equal intervals (6–9 points, Class A; 10–13, Class B; 14–15, Class C; 16–18, Class D), an equal number of children being selected to represent each class. Some changes in parental occupation and education took place during the course of the longitudinal study, so Family Background scores were recalculated on the basis of information obtained in the second parental interview. These recalculated scores were used in the present investigation but with the scale reversed so that Class A children received the highest scores and Class D the lowest. Measured in this way, Class of Family Background is found to be positively associated with educational attainment as estimated by tests ($r = .58$, $p<.001$) and teacher assessment ($r = .51$, $p<.01$); it also significantly distinguishes the High from the Low Attainers ($z = 3.01$, $p<.003$).

Towards a Developmental Model of Attainment

In reporting the results so far each of the antecedent variables has been treated as if its effect on educational attainment at seven years is direct and independent of each of the others. However this is clearly not the case. First the variables considered are not all of the same order: a score on a test, for example, represents a level of attainment reached by the child at a particular point in time, whereas parental interest in literacy, for example, is an attribute of people in the child's environment, which is assumed to have an effect through its influence on the actual interactions that take place between parents and child over a considerable period of time. It is thus closely related to other variables considered, such as the number of books owned by the child and the child's interest in literacy, in ways that are not captured by the simple correlations.

Secondly, not all of the variables represent factors which have a direct influence on educational attainment. High scores on the language profiles in the early years and characteristics of parental interaction with children at this age are of this kind. Positive correlations between these variables and educational attainment at seven years need to be interpreted in terms of the advantages of the early acquisition of a level of linguistic competence which enables the child to embark sooner on a qualitatively different range of activities and on the acquisition of new skills, some of which will be more directly related to educational attainment.

Thirdly, the effects are not always unidirectional. This is particularly true of the variables that measure attributes of the adults' contributions to interactions with their children. From studies of adult speech to language-learning children it is now well established that adults modify their speech to secure effective communication (Snow and Ferguson, 1977). Moreover, some of these modifications have been shown to be associated with the children's rate of language development (Furrow *et al.* 1979; Wells, 1980). However, particularly in the case of the most rapidly developing children, the parents 'tune' their speech quite finely in response to the level of comprehension manifested by the child (Cross, 1977) with the result that features of adult speech which may be facilitative of development in the early stages are gradually replaced by others in response to developments in the child's competence as a communicator.

Although not yet investigated to any significant extent, there are other characteristics of children which also seem likely to influence adult behaviour, for example their talkativeness, the sorts of topic that they introduce and their interest for an adult, and the way in which they participate in the interaction – for example, whether they ask many questions, whether they are argumentative and whether they provide positive feedback to the adult's contributions. Thus, although the types of behaviour, both verbal and non-verbal, that adults manifest when interacting with young children are clearly important as both model and feedback, it must be recognized that they do not occur independently of the behaviour of their children. If the conversations that the child experiences are facilitative of his or her further development, therefore, they are so as a result of interactions to which both child and adult contribute.

A longitudinal study such as the present one therefore requires a method of analysis which is sensitive to the complex interactions amongst the variables involved and which recognizes the cumulative nature of development – a continuous process in which there are nevertheless transitions to qualitatively different types of learning and behaviour, each having its own crucial antecedents. We are still far from having devised such a method; furthermore, many of the variables under consideration, particularly those derived from the interviews, are insufficiently precise for such an undertaking. Nevertheless, the first steps in this direction have been taken in a preliminary attempt to group the variables in relation to the most appropriate of a number of steps on the path towards attainment, as measured at seven years, with the steps being operationally defined by the four existing assessments of the children's language and academic attainment.

For this purpose correlations between these four sets of scores and the other predictor variables were calculated, with academic attainment at seven years being represented by the aggregate test scores alone, since these scores were judged to be more reliable than those derived from the teachers' assessments. The results of this analysis are presented in Figure 1.

The most striking feature of this analysis is the consistently and increasingly strong predictions which relate each step to the next along the path towards the last measurement of attainment at seven years, suggesting that some of the factors that affect differential attainment begin to operate at an early age. Although an inspection of the rank orders at each step shows that there are one or two children, who, despite a slow start in learning to talk, figure by the age of seven years amongst the high attainers, as there are also one or two whose early accelerated progress is not maintained as they make the transfer to school, in general these results seem to support the widely-held belief in a strong relationship between early language development and later educational attainment. There is also substantial evidence of the

Figure 1 Some antecedents of school attainment at age 7 years: a tentative model

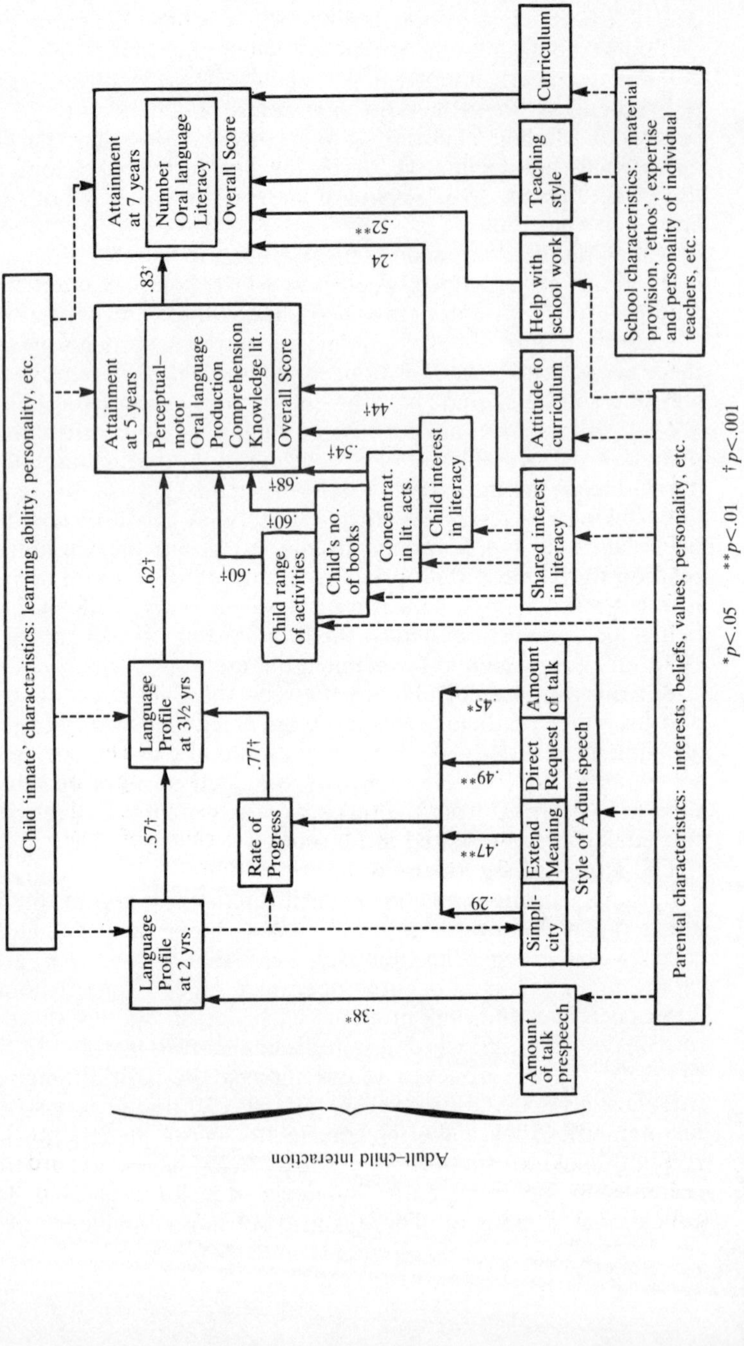

*p<.05 **p<.01 †p<.001

important role played by parents at every stage, but particularly in relation to the child's acquisition of the skills and attitudes which influence his or her educational attainment, as assessed in tests and similar situations. This finding, too, is entirely as expected.

The questions that have recently aroused such controversy, however, are first, whether there are class-associated differences in language development which are related to later educational attainment and, secondly, whether such differences involve some form of incompatibility between the language of home and school. To these questions the results reported here are not sufficient to provide clear-cut answers, although they do suggest the direction in which answers may be found.

As far as the association between social class and educational attainment is concerned, our results are similar to those reported elsewhere: at age seven there is a positive correlation of $r = .58$ ($p<.001$) with aggregate test scores and $r = .51$ ($p<.01$) with teacher assessment. On entry to school the obtained correlations were even higher, $r = .66$ on tests and $r = .63$ on teacher assessment. Yet the two earlier profiles of oral language ability do not show anything like such strong associations: $r = .24$ at two years and $r = .41$ at 3½ years, only the latter being statistically significant ($p<.05$).

Furthermore, inspection of the data shows that it is only a minority of extremely high and low scoring children on the latter profile of language ability who contribute to the obtained correlation, the remainder being distributed around the sample mean with no association between oral language ability and family background.

It might, nevertheless, be suggested that the increasing size of the correlations between two and 3½ years of age indicates a relationship which increases with age. The responses to the item in the first parental interview concerning the range of functions for which the children were judged by their parents to use language provides some support for such a suggestion. Scores on this item were significantly correlated both with tested attainment at age seven ($r = .44$, $p<.01$) and with family background ($r = .60$, $p<.001$). Although the functional categories that the parents were asked to consider in the interview were not identical to those used by Tough (1977), there was sufficient similarity between the two sets of categories for these results to be seen as offering some support for the importance she claims for this aspect of language use. On the other hand, in the earlier phase of the research programme, in which samples of spontaneous speech recorded at five years of age from a comparable group of 64 children were analysed in terms of the variables included in the language profiles already discussed, correlations between the various linguistic variables and family background were generally only in the order of $r = .3$, and, for the range of functions used, the correlation was only $r = .23$, which is not statistically significant. Furthermore, an attempt to apply Tough's categories to the spontaneous speech, recorded at 3½ years, of 32 of these children failed to show a clear pattern of class-related differences in the functional uses of language (Wells, 1977). Nevertheless, it is possible that such class-associated differences in language use only emerge in the later pre-school years. Until the analysis of the speech samples of the 32 children in the present study, recorded just prior to entry to school, has been completed, however, it is not possible to draw any conclusion on this issue.

Taking all the evidence from our longitudinal study into account, therefore, the general picture to have emerged so far is that, in the pre-school years at least, there is only a weak relationship between family background and oral language ability. Generalizing from these results, there is thus no reason to believe that the majority of lower class children suffer, on entry to school, from a serious deficiency in their control of the resources of the English language. On the uses that are habitually made of these resources our results to date are more equivocal. However, as will be argued below, it is in this area that class-related differences – if they occur – might be expected to be of the greatest significance for later educational attainment.

Qualitative Differences in the Children's Pre-School Linguistic Experience

The measures of oral language that have been considered so far are quantitative in nature. However, the stronger claims concern qualitative differences, either of code or of dialect. Such class-associated differences, it is argued, lead to an incompatibility between the language habitually used at home and that used at school, which is substantially greater for lower-class children.

The issue of regional, or non-standard, dialect and accent was addressed by means of the teacher assessments. On both occasions the teachers were asked to rate both the dialect and the accent of each child in terms of its closeness to standard English, using a three-point scale. Whilst there must certainly be some doubt about the reliability, in absolute terms, of ratings obtained in this way, it is probably just such judgements of departure from standard, relative to the teacher's expectations, that are important for individual children's progress in school, since what is at issue here is a matter of social acceptability, rather than one of mutual intelligibility.

The results of this analysis are interesting, but difficult to interpret. As expected, non-standard dialect and accent were found to be significantly negatively associated with family background. However the associations between non-standardness of dialect and accent, as assessed at age five, and attainment at age seven were relatively small and non-significant ($r = -.19$ for tests and $r = -.22$ for teacher assessment). On the other hand, the same questions about dialect and accent asked when the children were seven years old yielded ratings that showed a substantial negative association with the contemporaneous assessments of attainment ($r = -.52$, $p<.01$; $r = -.58$, $p<.001$). If these figures are to be accepted, it seems that the non-standard dialect or accent that is associated with low attainment is not a source of difficulty that results from some children having learned in the pre-school years a variety of language which is incompatible with that of the school, but rather a mark of group identity which is adopted or exaggerated after entering school, perhaps in response to their growing perception of themselves as low attainers.

A further type of possible incompatibility, which is related to dialect differences, concerns the relationship between pragmatic functions and the particular linguistic forms through which they are realized. It has been suggested, for example, that certain social groups may not be familiar with some of the forms that are used to make indirect requests or may not recognize the form of response that is required when a teacher asks a question to which she clearly already knows the answer. From our observations, however, it seems that the incidence and magnitude of such problems has been greatly exaggerated. As Sinclair and Coulthard (1975) point out, learning linguistic forms and learning social behaviour are inseparable in such cases, and children from all backgrounds are already adept at making the necessary connections as a result of their pre-school experience (Ervin-Tripp, 1980). In any case, as far as the form-function relationships are concerned that are most typical of classroom interaction, there do not appear to be major differences between social groups in what they have already learned at home. As MacLure and French comment at the conclusion of their comparison of the language experienced by the children in this study in the two settings of home and school:

> from the point of view of the child participants, from whatever social background, there is little in the nature of the interactional demands which will be made of children at school that they will not have become familiar with at home, at the level of conversational structure (1981, p.237).

The question as to whether there is a class-associated difference in the coding orientations of our subjects – children, parents and teachers – is not within our power to answer. Recent work within this framework has made it clear that codes are not directly observable but must be inferred from speech in context (Bernstein, 1977). To study the relationship between classes and codes, therefore, requires clear procedures for making the necessary inferences, and comparability of contexts in which the speech realizations are obtained. Our spontaneous speech data, however, do not permit a sufficiently close matching of contexts across children to allow valid comparisons to be made. Moreover, to have attempted to devise and apply the necessary coding frames would have exceeded our resources.

There are, in any case, reasons for doubting the appropriateness of treating the population as if it could be divided into two (or three) homogeneous social classes, middle and working (and/or lower-working), or of reducing the many parameters on which speech varies according to people's social and geographical origins and their perception of the context of interaction to two discrete underlying codes (Robinson, 1978). Certainly the language of the classroom cannot be contrasted with that of homes – whatever their social class – in terms of such a simple dichotomy.

To the extent that talk between teachers and pupils is different from that between parents and children at home, it is likely to be so for the great majority of pupils as a result of the asymmetry of control over speaking rights and criteria of relevance which is much more characteristic of curriculum-oriented interactions in the classroom than it is of most interaction in the home. However, the social and intellectual skills that pupils need in order to operate within the teacher's frame of reference go far beyond differences between home and school in the forms and functions of speech that are used in the two settings (Davies, 1980; Mehan, 1979).

As far as serious incompatibility is concerned, therefore, between the language spoken in the two settings of home and school, the evidence that lower-class children are at a much greater disadvantage than their middle-class peers does not seem to be particularly strong, at least for native speakers of English. At most there is some tendency, barely reaching a level of statistical significance, for lower-class children to be less advanced in their mastery of the common language, with socially based variations not being, in themselves, a major problem.

The Role of Literacy in Early Educational Attainment

What then is the reason for the substantial association between family background and attainment that appears as soon as the children enter the system of formal education? Doubtless, no one single factor is responsible, but in so far as linguistic differences do enter into the explanation, a closer examination of the tests administered on entry to school offers a clue as to where such differences may lie. As can be seen in Table 1, by far the most significant as a predictor of attainment at age seven is the test of Knowledge of Literacy. This suggests that, although an adequate mastery of spoken language is an important prerequisite for progress in school, it is knowledge and ability with respect to written language that is of particular importance.

Two reasons can be suggested for this. First, a major part of the curriculum in the early years of schooling is concerned with the acquisition of literacy, and ability in this area constitutes a large part of any assessment of attainment. Secondly, the skills involved in learning to read and write are characteristic of much of the learning that takes place at school in their relative abstractness and emphasis on the symbolic nature of linguistic representations. Talk at home typically arises out of immediate practical activity and is supported by the context in which it occurs; at school, on the other hand, direct contextual support for much of what is talked about is lacking and indeed, as Donaldson (1978) has argued, it is one of the chief aims of the school to help the child to 'disembed' his or her thinking from the supportive context of immediate experience and to bring it under the control of meanings that are encoded in the linguistic message alone. Clearly, learning to use the written language is one very important way of developing this ability. Not surprisingly, therefore, those children who already have some understanding of the purposes and organization of written language on entry to school are likely to have achieved a higher level of attainment two years later.

However, as our results show, this is very much dependent on the home environment and on the extent to which parents stimulate a general interest in books and reading, provide children with books of their own, and encourage them to persevere in their activities, particularly those associated with literacy. And this, in turn, is related to the value that the parents themselves place on literacy and the extent to which they have shared their own interests with their children, as is shown by the strong association between the separate measures of parents' and children's interest in literacy ($r = .74$, $p<.001$).

Now it is precisely in the area of literacy that substantial class-associated differences in the children's pre-school experience are found. As already stated, the associations between scores on the oral language profiles and family background were relatively small, and the same is true, speaking generally, of the quality of the adult speech addressed to the child in the early stages and of the amount of help given by parents with school work, although both are independently associated with the children's attainment at age seven. However, for all the variables concerned with literacy in the pre-school years, there is a strong association with family background, ranging from $r = .53$ in the case of number of books owned by the child to $r = .65$ for both the parents' and the children's interest in literacy.

It appears, therefore, that one important source of the class-associated differences that emerge in school-based assessments of attainment is the difference between homes in the value that is placed on literacy and in the steps that parents take to transmit this value to their children.

Perhaps even more important, however, is the pervasive effect of living in a home where the skills of literacy are used by the parents in their everyday activities, either at work or in their leisure pursuits. Where this is the case, it might be supposed, there will be a greater likelihood that, when appropriate, the exchange of meanings in conversation will be influenced by the more analytic manipulation of experience that is particularly characteristic of written language (Olson, 1977), with the result that the children have the opportunity to develop an awareness of the way in which language allows particular situations, problems and predicaments to be represented in symbolic categories and relations, which can be communicated about and acted upon independently of their context of origin. Such experience, it is suggested, allows them to begin to develop a facility with the 'disembedded' uses of language which are characteristic of much classroom talk and also of test situations, such as those in which attainment is formally assessed (Wells, 1981).

How far does the evidence support this speculation? Although the parental interviews had included questions about their own reading habits and about the extent to which they shared their interests in literacy with their children, no questions had been asked about the extent to which reading and writing influenced their spoken interactions with their children. Indeed, it is difficult to know how such information could be obtained by means of an interview. It is possible, however, to search the recordings of spontaneous conversation for manifestations of these forms of behaviour.

With this aim in view, the final home recordings of all 32

children made just before entry to school, were examined. Occurrences of three main categories of behaviour were tallied:

(a) manifestations of the child's interest in literacy – looking at books, attempting to write or asking questions about the meaning or written form of words;
(b) manifestations of the parents' encouragement of literacy – reading to the child, looking at a book or other written text with the child and talking about it, or giving help or instruction in reading or writing;
(c) manifestations of a move towards 'disembedded' use of language – the child considering hypothetical or imaginary situations or the parent enunciating general principles or conclusions, etc.

Whilst occurrences of (a) and (b) were relatively frequent and easy to recognize, with (c) it was much more difficult to be certain whether or not a particular stretch of conversation had moved beyond the immediate specific situation. A discussion of how the radio-microphone worked is a good example. In this case, since it was implied that all microphones worked in the same way, this was treated as the enunciation of a general principle. Some cases were more problematic. In the end it was decided to distinguish between certain and problematic examples and to give a score of 2 to the former and only 1 to the latter.

Scores for each of the three categories were calculated separately over the same amount of recorded time for each child. A total 'literacy influenced behaviour' score was also calculated by summing the three separate categories. Each of these sets of scores was then correlated with aggregate test scores at age five and with the family background scores. The results are shown in Table 2.

Table 2 Literacy behaviours × tests and family background

	Tests at 5	Family Background
Child interest in literacy	.44*	.34
Parents' encouragement of literacy	.13	.33
Disembedded uses of language	.35*	.29
Literacy influenced behaviour	.49**	.46**

*$p<.05$ **$p<.01$

As can be seen, the results are far from conclusive and, where comparisons can be made, the correlations are lower than with similar variables derived from the parents' interview responses. Although the combined score of 'literacy influenced behaviour' is significantly associated both with test scores at age five ($r = .49$, $p<.01$) and with family background ($r = .46$, $p<.01$), the disembedded use of language category alone is not significantly associated with family background ($r = .19$) and only barely so with tests at age five ($r = .35$, $p<.05$).

Several possible reasons can be suggested. First, the samples of recorded conversation (made up of 8 × 5 minutes), although long enough to contain instances of a wide range of linguistic categories, were not long enough to obtain a representative sample of large-scale activities and of the talk that might arise from such activities. Secondly, the recordings did not include the pre-bedtime period, when reading and related talk is most likely to occur. Thirdly, and most importantly as far as the probability of observing instances of disembedded talk is concerned, all the recordings took place inside the home and involved mainly rather routine activities. Talk that moves beyond the immediate context to a consideration of general principles and possibilities is probably most likely to occur, if it occurs at all, in relation to new and relatively unfamiliar events and situations, such as would be more likely to be encountered on expeditions outside the home. Clearly, a study designed specifically to test the hypothesized relationships will be necessary before any firm conclusions can be drawn about the influence of parental literacy on the quality of parent–child conversation in the home and, as a result, on the child's preparedness for formal education.

However, with respect to the more general influence of pre-school experience of literacy on early educational attainment and of the association between such experience and family background, these results can be seen as providing corroboration for those already discussed. Taken together, they leave little doubt about the importance that the mastery of the written language has for early school attainment, both as curriculum content in the first stage of schooling, and in the more reflective and analytic attitude to the relationship between language and experience that using the written language both requires and encourages. They also suggest that, in so far as familiarity with the functions of written language has an effect on the quality of conversation in the home, this will also be associated with family background.

It may be suggested that the emphasis on learning to disembed one's thinking from the immediate context of experience is not very dissimilar to the characteristics that Bernstein associates with orientation to an elaborated code. Certainly, the theoretical model that he offers to account for the social transmission of knowledge and values is one which I have found, in general terms, to be extremely stimulating. However, whilst being willing to accept the relationship between educational achievement and the ability, gradually acquired through experience of interaction in the home, to recognize contexts in which it is appropriate to organize meanings in a way which is not tied to the immediate context – hence 'universalistic' in tendency – I am unwilling, for the reasons already given, to subscribe to the dichotomization of either the organization of society or the characterization of habitual styles of speech, or to the deterministic linking of class and code. The evidence from the longitudinal study of a broadly representative sample of families, on part of which this chapter is based, points to a very substantial similarity in the early conversational experience of children across all classes of family background; however, it also indicates that there are many parameters on which there is variation between individual families in what is made salient in the course of everyday interaction.

The importance attached to literacy is one such parameter and one that, it has been suggested, has a significant relationship both with the children's educational attainment and with family background. That this should be so is not surprising, since family background was assessed in this study on the basis of the parents' type of occupation and their terminal level of education, both of which are intimately related to the extent of their mastery and use of the written language. In a society which affords high status and financial reward to occupations which demand a high level of literacy, it is to be expected that those who have achieved such status will be anxious to transmit the same skills to their children.

It is not, of course, being suggested that differential familiarity with the functions and values of literacy is the only – or even the most important – influence on educational attainment. Although not examined in this study, differences between families in parental understanding of, and concurrence with, the aims and methods of primary education, on the one hand, and in the material provision and the expectations of teachers in the schools that serve them, on the other, are wider in scope and more pervasive in their effect than differences relating only to literacy. Nevertheless, since attainment within our educational system is highly dependent on the mastery of skills that are particularly associated with written language, it seems possible that the relationship between family background and educational attainment in the early years may be quite largely mediated by class-associated differences in the relative salience that is given to activities associated with literacy in interaction between parents and children.

Conclusion

The results reported here represent the first stage of a longitudinal analysis of the language-related antecedents of early educational attainment. They show that, whilst academic attainment at age seven is to some extent dependent on the level of a child's oral language ability on entry to school, and that this, in turn, is associated with the quality of linguistic interaction experienced during the pre-school years, an adult style of conversation that facilitates the development of oral language is not, in itself, sufficient to equip a child to benefit from the opportunities for learning provided by the more formal context of the classroom. Familiarity with more abstract and less context-dependent uses of language, such as those associated with written text, seem to be of even greater importance, and this tends to be associated with the place and value of literacy in the everyday life of the parents, which, in turn, is associated with their own educational and occupational experience. Where this familiarity is absent, children are at a disadvantage both because they lack skills which are important for learning in school and also because this lack of skills affects the ways in which their teachers interact with them.

The variables considered here have been chiefly those derived from the pre-school data and the emphasis has been on differences between children in their readiness for school. However this should not be taken to imply that children's differential experiences at school are of little significance in accounting for later attainment. Whilst there was very great similarity in the responses that the teachers gave to questions about the ways in which they organized the curriculum, individual case-studies reveal substantial differences between them in the ways in which they actually interacted with individual children in the realization of their curricular objectives (Wells and Montgomery, 1981), and in due course we hope to be able to include variables derived from the classroom observations in the longitudinal analysis.

Where learning takes place chiefly through linguistic interaction, as it clearly does in the early years, the style of interaction that a child habitually experiences can be expected to have an important influence on the learning strategies and attitudes that he develops. And whilst it is important to emphasize that the conversational context of learning is a joint creation, built up of meanings and intentions contributed by both child and adult participants, it is clear that the adult has a particularly influential role – either facilitating or constraining – in shaping that context. Our own findings show this to be the case for the pre-school years, and work being carried out elsewhere (Cook-Gumperz *et al.*, 1979; Schultz *et al.*, 1982) suggests that the same is true of the early years of schooling. In seeking to understand the antecedents of early educational attainment, therefore, we need to examine not only the knowledge and skills that children bring to the learning situation, but also the patterns of interaction through which they are introduced to particular tasks and helped to bring their knowledge and skills to bear in carrying them out.

CHAPTER 6
Talking with Children: the Complementary Roles of Parents and Teachers

At the age of five, all children in our culture reach an important milestone in their development, as they move from the familiar and supportive environment of their home into the larger unknown world of school. During the next ten years the aim of those who teach them will be to induct them into the skills, knowledge and values of the wider culture, and to help them to achieve independence and responsibility in the use of their individual talents, both contributing to, and receiving from, the social, intellectual and material resources of the society of which they are becoming members. However, some children benefit from their schooling much more than others, and it has frequently been argued that a major cause of differential success is the difference between children as a result of their pre-school linguistic experience at home in the ability to meet the linguistic expectations of the classroom.

Certainly, language must play a large part in the ease or difficulty with which children make the transition from home to school. For the many differences between the two environments – in size, in organization patterns and routines, in the goals that are set and in the means that children are expected to use in achieving them – impinge most strongly on the child's moment-by-moment experience through the differences in styles of linguistic interaction that characterize them. The greater the difference, the more likely it is that the child will experience a sense of disorientation, which may manifest itself in behaviour that is assessed as lack of ability or unwillingness to learn. Once labelled in this way, it may become progressively more difficult for such children to overcome their initial disadvantage and reach the levels of achievement of which they are potentially capable.

In spite of much theorizing on this subject, however, there has been very little systematic study of the actual experience of children making this crucial transition, apart from the studies of Bernstein (1973) and Tough (1977), which have observed children in quasi-experimental situations in school and then either inferred the characteristics of home experience which preceded the performance in school or drawn obliquely upon questionnaire information. The Bristol study, 'Language at Home and at School' is probably unique in following a representative sample of children through the pre-school years and into the infant school, recording regular samples of their spontaneous use of language in these two settings. In this chapter, I shall try to describe some of the main characteristics of children's experience of talk at home and at school, as we have observed it in the recordings we have made, and I shall consider some of the implications of the differences that emerge from a comparison between them for the ease with which children make the transition.

Talk at Home

If one asked parents the question 'Why should children talk?', one would probably receive an answer such as that given by one particular mother: 'It's natural. They want to join in and be like other people. They just learn from listening to and talking to other people'. And in many ways, 'naturalness' describes what we have observed. Despite wide variations in the kinds of home in which they are growing up, there is remarkable uniformity in the sequence in which children learn the main components of language and even in the rate at which this learning takes place. There are differences between children, of course, both in the age at which they begin to talk and in the stage they have reached on entry to school, but these are relatively insignificant when compared with the amount that all children learn in these early years. All but a very small minority of children reach the age of schooling with a vocabulary of several thousand words, control of the basic grammar of the language of their community, and an ability to deploy these resources in conversation arising from the many and varied situations that occur in their everyday lives. Of all the children that we have studied, there is only one of whom this claim cannot be made with confidence, and even he is by no means limited to 'a basically non-logical mode of expressive behaviour', as Bereiter (1966) would have us believe to be typical of vast numbers of children. It seems, therefore, that the child's predisposition to learn whatever language he is exposed to, together with some minimum experience of language in use, is sufficient for the child to acquire a basic linguistic competence before he goes to school.

However, there are important differences between children,

particularly when looked at from the point of view of the transition to school, and these concern the uses they habitually make of their linguistic resources: the things they talk about and the ways in which they talk about them (Halliday, 1968). Learning one's native language is not simply a matter of learning vocabulary and grammar, but rather of learning to construct shared meanings as part of collaborative activities in which the words and sentences both refer to the shared situation and reflect a particular orientation to it. As Bernstein (1971) has argued, through the aspects of common experience that parents choose to talk about, and particular relations that are given prominence in the form of their utterances, they present to their children a particular view of the world and their place within it. For example, if objects are constantly referred to in terms of ownership, and prohibitions and permissions are justified in terms of proprietorial rights, the child will be quick to learn the grammatical markers of possession (Wells, 1974) and over time will acquire an orientation to 'property' that is very different from that of the child whose parents encourage an exploratory attitude to objects, only prohibiting an interest in particular objects when there is a risk of danger.

Differences of orientation resulting from parental emphasis are particularly common between the sexes, boys and girls being subtly directed towards different interests through the situations in which their parents choose to initiate conversations with them. In a comparison we made of conversations initiated with three-year-olds, we found that over half the conversations with girls were in relation to household activities where the children were frequently 'helping' to carry out the task (a ratio of 2:1 compared with the boys), whereas a far greater proportion of conversations with boys were in situations where the children were engaged in exploratory play, with or without the active participation of the adult (a ratio of 3.5:1). Surprisingly enough, there were not such marked differences between boys and girls in the conversation that they initiated at this age, but by the time children start school, there are quite strong differences between boys and girls in the topics that they most frequently talk about – differences that are at least partly the result of their earlier experiences at home.

There are differences, too, in the ways in which language contributes to the structuring of experience. Everything that happens in a child's daily life is a potential subject for the sort of talk that facilitates attention, interpretation and evaluation, but parents differ in the use they make of these opportunities. In some homes, events are taken very much for granted, each one receiving

The Complementary Roles of Parents and Teachers

the same sort of passing comment, whereas in other homes there is a much greater selectivity, some events being discussed in considerable detail and connections made with the wider context in which they occur. As a result of such different experiences, the internal models of the world that children are constructing take on their particular shapes and textures and come to be more fully developed in some areas than others.

In the following episodes we can see these subtle shaping processes in action as particular events are explored through talk. In the first example, James (aged 3½ years) has just come in from playing outside, and he is standing at the door, taking his boots off. He draws his mother's attention to a bird, and his mother takes up his interest, explaining the bird's nest-building activities.

M: There we are [M helping J to change]
There – one slipper on

J: I can see a bird

M: A what, love? [J watching bird in garden]

J: See a bird

M: Is there? Outside? (whispers)

J: Yes (whispers)
J: See (whispers) [J points to bird]

M: Is he eating anything? (whispers)

J: No (whispers)

M: Where? (whispers throughout)

M: Oh yes he's getting –
Do you know what he's doing?

J: No (whispers)

M: He's going to the . .
the . . paper sack to try and pick out some pieces –
Oh he's got some food there
And I expect he'll pick out some pieces of thread from the sack to go and make

         his nest . . up . .
         underneath the roof,
         James
         Wait a minute and
         I'll –
         OK wait a mo – wait a
         mo James
J: That bird's gone
  (whispers)
       M: Has it gone now?
J: Yes (whispers)
       M: Oh
         Take those long
         trousers off because
         they're . . a bit
         muddy in there

Here we see a mother naturally entering into her child's interest and directing it through the fuller meaning she gives to what they are looking at together.

In the second example, Wendy (aged 3½ years) is playing at the kitchen sink.

W: I'm going to   [W climbs onto
  play with the   a chair at the]
  water again,   sink]
  Mummy
  Is that all right?
      . . 6 . .
             [M returns to
             kitchen]
W: I'm washing this
  for you, Mummy
       M: You're being very
         helpful this morning,
         Wendy
         (appreciatively)
         Er. Yes (doubtfully)
         Don't make it TOO
         bubbly, love
             [M comes to
             investigate]

The Complementary Roles of Parents and Teachers   105

	Have you put some more – ?	[Refers to wash-up liquid]
	No (= don't do that) 'Cos Mummy's just wiped up all that, lovey And I told you I didn't want to get it too wet Didn't I?	
W: I want to play –		
	M: Er – no	
		[M wipes draining board again]
	There we are Now try NOT to get all the water over there, love Please	
	. . 19 . .	
		[M continues to wipe and put away dishes. W blows bubbles through a straw]
W: See those bubbles! Come and see those bubbles		
	M: Just a minute, love And I'll come right away	

This time the child's interest doesn't entirely fit in with Mother's plans, but the mother accepts the child's intentions before setting restraining conditions on how the activity can be carried out.

Finally, Jacqueline at the much younger age of 2¼ years brings a book to show to her mother.

J: Look at those balls, Mum I show you	
	[Jacq. holds out book]
M: Show me what, darling?	

J: I show you all the
    balls
    I show you balls
    M: You're showing me
      the balls in your book,
      are you?
      Let me see then
      Where?
J: Balls   [Jacq. shows the picture]
    M: What's this?   [M asks about other picture]
J: That's doggy
    M: What's this?
J: That's a pussy cat
    M: And who's this?
J: That's Lulu
    M: Hasn't she got a lovely kitten?
J: Lulu's putting the
    – Pussy cat's
    M: Lulu's putting the pussy cat's hat on, yes
J: Lulu's – pussy cat's
    Lulu's – putting pussy cat's hat on

  Mother's questions here are first to check that she has understood the child's intentions correctly and then to invite her to go on talking about the pictures. We can see here how the mother guesses Jacqueline's meaning intention and provides her with the complete form, which Jacqueline is then able to say herself.
  In all these examples of 'home-talk' we can see a number of important qualities that characterize the sort of conversational experience which leads to effective use of language by children:

1. A warm responsiveness to the child's interests and a recognition of the child as an autonomous individual with valid purposes and ways of seeing things.
2. Negotiation of meaning and purpose in the joint construction of an inter-subjective reality.
3. An invitation to the child to consider the immediate present in a wider framework of intention and consequence, feeling and principles.

Such conversations also have, albeit loosely and sometimes imperfectly, a reciprocity and cohesion which results from both participants attempting to understand the meaning intended by the other and to express their own meanings in ways which will be understood against the background of shared information that has either been made explicit or can be taken for granted.

There are a number of further characteristics which distinguish such talk from that which is most typical of schools. First most of the conversations are initiated by the child (70 per cent was the figure we found in one analysis); secondly, it is sporadic, arising spontaneously from the interest of the moment, and it is almost completely lacking in a didactic pressure to teach particular facts or skills; and thirdly, it ranges widely over the whole of the family's shared experience, both inside and outside the home.

Talk at School

All the children quoted above are making excellent progress at school. Indeed, Jacqueline has made such good progress that she has been moved into the junior school well before her seventh birthday, and James is the most advanced reader of the children we have been following up in the project 'Children Learning to Read'. The following extract, which shows how confidently Jacqueline is coping with the routines of school life, is taken from a recording made when she had been in school less than a term. She has just drawn a picture of Jack Frost, and is about to dictate a story to go with it.

```
                        T:  What're we going to
                            write here today?
J:  This . is . a –                             [Jacq. dictates
                                                 to T]
B:  Jack
J:  No
                        T:  What's his name?    [Jacq. plays with
                                                 T's pendant]
J:  Jack Frost
                        T:  Jack Frost
J:  Here . is . Jack                            [Jacq. dictates
    Frro-                                        to T]
                        T:  Jack                [T writing]
                            What's Jack Frost
                            doing?
J:  Frosting the grass
```

108   *Language, Learning and Education*

		T:	He . is . frosting. He's frosting the grass [Jacq. continues to dictate]
J:	With –		
		T:	With – oh with whom?
J:	His wand		
		T:	With his wand (sounding surprised) What's he doing to you? [Jacq. looks at her fingers]
J:	Nibbling my toes and my – and fingers		
		T:	He's nibbling?
J:	Yeh		
		T:	Nibbling? Right
J:	My . toes –		
		T:	Nibbling – [T writing]
J:	– and my –		
		T:	– my –
J:	– fingers		[Jacq. holds up her fingers]
		T:	And my – ? What else did you say?
J:	Chin		
		T:	Chin Oh you're going to write – Have to write this line very little, won't you? Now . d'you remember how you did it?
J:	Yeh		
		T:	That line goes along there [T shows Jacq. in which direction to write]
J:	Yeh (= Yes, I know)		
		T:	Do you want me to put the dots for you or can you do it without the dots?

J: I can do it
   without the dots
   (with assurance)

The final story, which was written with great concentration, read as follows:

> Here is Jack Frost.
> He is frosting the grass with his wand.
> He is nibbling my toes, my fingers and my chin.

From Jacqueline's point of view, it seems that the answer to our question 'Why should children talk?' is that it is both enjoyable and interesting. She has confidence, because her experience has led her to form expectations that people will take her seriously as a conversational partner and will be interested in what she has to say. And indeed, watching her with her teacher, it seems that her expectations are justified.

Not all children make the transition to school so easily, however, and some, lacking confidence and fluency, may be so tongue-tied and monosyllabic that they give the impression of being almost without language altogether. Teachers certainly have the impression that many children enter school with a 'linguistic deficit', and those who are unwilling or unable to respond to the linguistic demands of the classroom apparently lend support to this impression. How serious, then, is the problem? Certainly there are children who have little or no command of English on entry to school, but these are, almost without exception, children of non-English-speaking parents: their problem is not lack of language, but lack of English, and they need the special provision of appropriate opportunities for second language learning. These children apart, the number of children of English-speaking parents who have not acquired a basic command of English by the age of five is very small indeed. However, the particular dialect of English they have learnt, or the uses they habitually make of language, may be different from those most valued in school, and as a result, they may find it difficult to communicate successfully with strange adults, who are unfamiliar with their expectations.

Differences resulting from non-standard dialects need not be a handicap, for they rarely cause serious misunderstanding; and as Labov (1970) and others have demonstrated, they are in no sense linguistically inferior to the standard dialect. Differences in habitual use of language, on the other hand, can have much more serious consequences, because behaviour resulting from difference

110 *Language, Learning and Education*

can so easily be mistaken for deficiency. The following example, recorded at the end of Rosie's first month in school, is a good example of the sort of difficulties that can occur.

A small group of children are looking at colour slides of India. The teacher has selected a slide, looked at it through the viewer, and passed it to Rosie.

		T:	They're Indian ladies, and what else?	[R look through viewer]
R:	I can see something			
		T:	What can you see?	
R:	And they're going in the sand			
		T:	Mm?	[T fails to understand]
R:	You have a look			[R hands viewer to T]
		T:	Well you have a look and you tell me I've seen it already I want to see if you can see	[T hands viewer back to R]
			. . 6 . .	[R look through viewer]
R:	Oh they're going in the sand They're going in the sand			
				[T doesn't hear as she is attending to other children]
			. . 20 . .	
		T:	What's behind the men? Can you see the men in the red coats?	
. .				[R still looking]
		T:	Can you see the men in the red coats? What is behind . those men?	
			. . . .	
		T:	Can you see?	

The Complementary Roles of Parents and Teachers

R: They're walking in –
T: Pardon?
R: They're walking
T: They're walking, yes
But what's walking behind them?
Something very big
R: A horse
T: It's much bigger than a horse
It's much much bigger than a horse
It's big and grey and it's got a long nose that we call a trunk   [T mimes a long trunk]
R: Trunk (imitating)
T: Can you see what it is? What is it?
R: (nods)
C: (unintelligible)
T: No that's what his nose is
Its nose is called a trunk
Can you see what the animal is?
R: N – no (= I can't guess)
T: It's much bigger than a horse
Let's give it to Darren and see if Darren knows
. . 20 . .   [D looks. R puts her thumb in her mouth. T looks for more pictures in books.]

112 *Language, Learning and Education*

```
                         T:  There's a picture of the
                             animal that was
                             walking behind the
                             men – with the red
                             coats on
                             What's that?            [T shows picture
                                                      to R]
R:  The soldiers
                         T:  Mm?
R:  Soldiers  ⎫
D:  Elephant  ⎬ (simultaneously)
              ⎭
                         T:  What's that             [T points to the
                                                      elephant]
R:  An elephant
```

The complete episode lasts almost five minutes and one hardly knows who is most deserving of sympathy – child or teacher. The teacher, apparently assuming that Rosie can produce the desired answer, gives her as many clues as possible, but all to no avail, for Rosie consistently adopts strategies unhelpful to the task as posed by the teacher, such as inviting the teacher to look, and describing only the people in the picture. Given her final response, it is difficult to know if she knew the word 'elephant'; but whether she did or not, she clearly did not perceive the task as one where she was required to produce this word or to admit her ignorance and ask for information.

It is interesting to contrast this episode with a somewhat similar conversation between Rosie and her mother that arose in the course of doing the housework. (See the example quoted *ante* at p.18.) Here again a question was asked to which Rosie did not know the answer, but once her mother had realized this, she provided the answer herself and Rosie echoed it with enthusiasm.

The point of making this comparison, however, is not to claim that Rosie's mother is more effective as a teacher, or even as a conversation partner, for in most ways she is not. What is brought out by the comparison is the relatively greater control of the language system that Rosie displays at home, and particularly when she initiates the interchange. One must conclude, therefore, that Rosie's failure to meet the linguistic demands of her teacher is not an absolute lack of language skills, as one might suppose if one simply met her at school, but rather that her poor performance is in part due to the nature of the demands made on her at school, particularly their remoteness from direct, personal involvement in a shared or self-initiated activity.

The Complementary Roles of Parents and Teachers

It has become fashionable to lay the blame for the sort of ineptitude that Rosie displays in the school episode above on the inadequacies of the home environment, and in some cases this may be appropriate, at least in part. Rosie is indeed one of the least linguistically mature children in our sample, and her home, although a place of much warmth and concern for the children's happiness, is not one where the sort of conversation that was illustrated in the first section of this paper is at all frequent. Nevertheless, as we have just seen, even such children may have linguistic abilities that are not called forth by the particular range of demands that are made on them in school, and so it is their deficiencies rather than their abilities which are most salient to their teachers. Such children are doubly unfortunate, and there is no doubt that there are substantial numbers of them. However, any suggestion that working class children *as a whole* are 'disadvantaged', in any absolute or irrevocable sense, because their home experience leads them to use language differently, is certainly not appropriate. A comparison of 40 children from our study (Wells, 1977) drawn from the full social spectrum, showed that there were not clear-cut differences between classes in the use of language, such as those found by Joan Tough (1977) in her study of groups selected to represent the extremes of social class. Of the three children whose 'home-talk' was illustrated earlier, two were from working-class homes (Jacqueline and James), and neither showed any signs of linguistic disadvantage either on entry to school or later.

As well as being inaccurate, such sweeping assertions about the inadequacies of homes have the additional disadvantage of distracting teachers from their obligation to examine their own role in helping children to make a success of the transition from home to school. We have seen an example which illustrates how some children fail to meet the linguistic demands of schools. But are the demands themselves entirely appropriate, either to the children who are entering school or to the longer-term aims of education that are espoused by the majority of teachers?

In order to pursue this question further, let us next consider some typical examples of classroom interaction selected from the observations we have been making of children during their first term in school.

In the first extract, the teacher has read *Little Black Sambo* and is recapitulating the main points of the story with the whole class:

> T: He would feel fat,
> wouldn't he, after
> eating all those?

Chn: Yes
C_1: He would burst
>T: He would burst, yes
>What did the first tiger take off Little Black Sambo?

C_1: Shirt
C_2: His coat
>T: His coat that his mummy had made
>Do you remember when his mummy made it?
>What colour was it?

Chn: Red
>T: Red, yes
>What did the second tiger take?

Chn: Trousers
>T: His trousers
>What did the third tiger take?

Chn: Shoes
>T: Was he pleased to take the shoes?

Chn: Yes
>No
>T: Why not?

C_1: Because he had 40 feet
>T: He said – what did he say to him?

C_2: I've got four feet and you've**
>T: I've got four feet and you've got –?

Chn: Two
>T: You haven't got enough shoes for me

In the second extract, the teacher has arranged a small group to do number work: counting beads and threading them on to a string with number labels. Penny is working faster than the other members of the group:

P: I'm winning [P is threading coloured beads on to a string to match number cards]

T: I'll come and see if they're right

P: One two three four five six seven

T: That's right [T Checks P's work]
What's after seven?

P: Eight

T: Eight
Can you find another [Telling P to eight? find a number card with 8 on]

P: Can you see a number eight?

T: I can see one two [P picks a card three four number with 8 in green] eight

T: That's right
What colour have you got to find this time?

P: Blue

T: Blue

The third extract once again comes from a session involving the whole class, following the reading of *Elmer the Elephant*. In the course of a discussion of some of the pictures, Stella volunteers a personal anecdote:

T: Can you see what that elephant's got on the end of his trunk?

Chn: (laugh)

T: What is it?

Chn: A blower

T: A blower – a party blower
It is funny, isn't it?

S: My – my – my
brother brought
one home from a
party

    T: Did he?
What does it do as well
as blowing?

S: Um
C₁: (inaudible)

    T: Sh!   [T signals she
What does it do?   wants S to
    answer

S: Mm – the thing   [S makes an
rolls out   appropriate
    gesture]

    T: Yes the thing rolls
down and rolls up
again, doesn't it?
But what does it do as
well as unrolling and
rolling up?

S: Um

    T: Does it do anything
else?

C₁: Squeaks

    T: Sh!   [T signals for S
Does Adrian's   to answer]
squeak?–
Adrian's blower
squeak?

S: (nods)

    T: Does it?
They usually squeak
and they often have a
little feather on it too,
don't they?   [Intonation of
    finality]

Chn: Yes (chanted)

    T: Well I think that's a
lovely story
It's one of my
favourite ones

The Complementary Roles of Parents and Teachers 117

The first thing that strikes one about these episodes – unless one already takes it for granted – is the very high proportion of teacher utterances that are questions, and of these what a very small proportion are questions to which the teachers do not already know the answer. Even when the form of the question seems to invite a variety of answers, there is often only one that is really acceptable to the teacher, and it is not uncommon to see children gazing at the teacher's face in an effort to guess what is in her mind, down to the precise word. It almost seems from these examples that teachers believe the answer to the question about why children should talk to be 'because teachers ask them questions'.

However, as we saw in the examples of 'home-talk', one of the chief characteristics of effective conversation is a reciprocity in the shared construction of meaning. Questions do occur but to nothing like the same extent as in the school examples and – more importantly – when they do occur they are asked equally by child and adult, and almost always because the asker is seeking information which he believes the hearer can supply. Many teacher-directed questions, on the other hand, show very little evidence of reciprocity: the asker already possesses the requested information and seems, as often as not, to direct the question to the pupil who is least likely to know the answer. It is true that most children will already have had some experience of questions of this sort in specific contexts such as identifying objects in picture books, or learning nursery rhymes by heart. But what about those children who are not at all familiar with the rules of this particular language game? They will, of course, eventually have to learn them in order to fit in at higher levels of education where the 'closed question' and the 'Teacher Initiation – Pupil Response – Teacher Feedback' routine have been shown to be the norm (Barnes, 1971; Sinclair and Coulthard, 1975). But in the shorter term the bewildering experience of being judged according to their ability to play a game whose rules are completely unfamiliar to them may persuade them once and for all that school is an alien institution and the activities that take place there are both irrelevant to their model of social interaction and destructive of the self-confidence that they have built up in their ability to talk within the rules that operate at home.

Even in the longer term, is the style of interaction exemplified in the 'school-talk' above conducive to the generally agreed aims of education? How far does it contribute to the independent, active and inquiring attitude that is essential if pupils are, as Barnes (1976) puts it, to convert 'school' knowledge into 'action' knowledge, and make it the basis for further learning? What preparation does it provide for the reciprocal negotiation of meaning that every adult needs to be able to engage in, in their many dealings with other people in social groups, at work and in their contacts with bureaucracy? Just as young children's internal models of reality are shaped by the salience that is given to different aspects of experience in their conversations with their parents, so does the pupil's model of reality continue to be shaped by those orientations to knowledge and those styles of interpersonal interaction that are given salience in the transactions of the classroom. That being so, the domination of school-talk by the teacher-evaluator, and the constant pressure on the pupil to produce correct verbal responses as acceptable tokens of the thought processes that the curriculum is designed to encourage, can hardly be the most effective way to achieve the goals that are set.

This is not to argue, however, that infant schools should attempt to replicate the style of interaction that typifies the best sort of home. Even if there were agreement on what is the best sort of home, such an aim would be neither appropriate nor feasible. Although both home and school have an educational function, the school complements the informality of the home by introducing the child to more formal ways of acquiring and utilizing knowledge, and its organization draws upon the skills of highly trained and expensive professionals. I do not, therefore, intend to suggest that teachers can substantially change the imbalance between their own and pupil's share of pupil–teacher interaction (not at least without a prohibitively expensive increase in the teacher–pupil ratio), nor do I wish to suggest that teachers should give up asking questions. What I do wish to suggest is that they should be much more flexible in their style of interaction, selecting the type of teacher–pupil talk that is best suited to the purpose of the particular activity that the pupils are engaged in.

Talk in Relation to Tasks

Since most of what goes on in the classroom is designed to contribute to some part of the overall curriculum, it may be helpful to think of most of the activities that children engage in in terms of *Tasks*, each task having a *Goal* with respect to some area of the curriculum that provides its *Content*. For example, Penny's activity of bead-threading above is just such a task. The goal of this task is to produce a sequence of groups of beads that matches the numbers and colours on the instruction cards: the content is foundation work for mathematics. Naturally, particular tasks may

The Complementary Roles of Parents and Teachers 119

be relevant to more than one area of the curriculum, and there are a variety of ways of dividing the curriculum into content areas, depending on the purpose of the division. However, for this discussion I should like to make a broad distinction between four broad areas: skills, knowledge, values and creative activities, and I shall argue that the sorts of goals that are set, and the procedures that are appropriate for attaining them, differ according to which of the content areas is involved.

Language enters into tasks to varying extents, sometimes as no more than a relatively unimportant procedure, as for example when the child needs to ask a neighbour for some object that is required to complete a task that is being carried out individually and sometimes as the goal of the task itself, as for example in individual writing or in class discussion. In general, except where language skills provide the content of the task, the degree to which language is central is least in the area of skills and it increases towards the creative activities end of the continuum, except where the creative activities are essentially non-linguistic. However, when a task of any kind involves talk between teacher and child, the style of talk that occurs carries messages about the interpersonal relationship between them and about the teacher's orientation to the content of the talk as well as messages about the task itself.

From this point of view, perhaps the most important dimension on which tasks differ is the extent to which the goal of the task is determined in advance.

The goal of an addition task, for example, is normally entirely predetermined: 2+2 = 4, and no other outcome is acceptable, once the procedure of addition has been fully grasped. The creation of a picture or imaginary story, on the other hand, has initially an almost entirely undetermined goal, although procedural criteria of internal consistency and practical skills in manipulating brush or pencil may be relevant in assessing the way in which the goal is realized, once this has been fully decided. Between these two extremes, there are varying degrees of constraint on the form that the outcome of a task may take, and on the procedures that are appropriate in arriving at it. However, the decision as to where a particular task falls along this continuum is very much in the hands of teachers, through the way in which they present the task and the style of talk they adopt in their own contribution to its achievement.

With this rough sketch of a framework for thinking about tasks, we are now in a better position to consider the kinds of talk that are appropriate to tasks of different kinds. Let us start with a type of task where the strategy of 'closed' questioning *is* appropriate.

120 *Language, Learning and Education*

The first example is taken from a study of language in the infant school carried out by Margaret Hocking (1977). The task involves the concepts of 'older' and 'younger', and the procedure suggested is a comparison of pairs of children with respect to their month of birth. The teacher is calling the children to her, two at a time. Here she is talking to Sarah and Lawrence:

	T: Right, which is the oldest?
S: I am	
	T: Let's see which is the eldest of you two?
L: Sarah	
	T: (to S) Now your birthday came in January You were seven in January What were you Sarah?
S: Seven	
	T: Who's the eldest?
L: Me	
	T: Who do you think is the eldest? (to S)
S: (inaudible)	
	T: You think Lawrence is the eldest, do you?
S: Yes	
	T: Now think about it Yours was January Lawrence came in February Which is the eldest?
S: Lawrence, I think	
	T: Well who came first?
S: I did	
	T: Then I think you are probably the eldest, don't you? You go at the top then Put it on the top one [Sarah puts her name at the top of the ladder]

L: I'm the second [Lawrence places his name underneath]

The second example comes from a study being carried out by Jan Adams, as part of our research programme, in which the aim is to compare the teaching styles of parents and teachers. The child is given a collection of picture-cards of familiar objects, including the members of a family, items of clothing, toys, foods, etc. The task presented to the child is that of grouping the pictures of things that go together, but no constraint is put upon the criteria that may be used in forming groups. The teacher's (or parent's) role is to help the child to apply whatever criterion he or she chooses in a consistent manner, and to discuss the criterion where this is helpful. In the example we see Rosie, the child quoted earlier, carrying out the task with her teacher.

T: Let's have a good look at some of the pictures
Can you tell me what's here?
Can you tell me some of the things that are here?

R: That's a swing

T: Which one is a swing? [T points to picture of swing]
This one?

R: (nods)

T: What do you do to a swing?

R: Sit on it

T: Can you find some other things that you can sit on?

R: Yes

T: Have a look and see if you can find some other things that you sit on and we'll put all of those together with the swing

R: Ain't nothing else

R: There's a bike

R: (nods)

T: What about these? [T points to several pictures] [R picks up bike]

T: Can you sit on a bike?

T: Put it with the swing then

Both of these examples (together with the earlier examples of Penny threading beads) have a number of features in common. First, they are taken from tasks which have clearly understood goals with respect to content, on the border between skills and knowledge; both also involve clear cut procedures – comparison of birth-date in the first, and classification according to a chosen criterion in the second – in order to achieve those goals. Secondly, because they are based on particular items of publicly available knowledge, they fall at the end of the continuum where the outcome is relatively predetermined, and applications of the procedures can be appropriately described as right or wrong. Thirdly, the teacher is using these particular instances as examples of very general principles; fourthly, implicit in the task-related dialogue, is the expectation that the child will internalize the procedure embodied in the question-and-answer sequence, so that she will eventually be able to operate such procedures alone, with the aid of a similar, internal, dialogue. The relationship between teacher and pupils on these tasks might therefore be aptly described as that between master and apprentice, and the dialogue as a means of increasing the pupils' awareness of the appropriate procedures for manipulating available information to achieve an agreed goal. However, these goals are essentially instrumental, since they concern skills that should eventually function as procedures in higher order tasks.

If we now turn to the sort of task represented by the discussion of *Elmer the Elephant*, we can see that it is of a very different kind. Here the point of departure is the shared class experience of listening to the story of Elmer the elephant, and the particular task we are concerned with is initiated by Stella's spontaneous contribution, sparked off by mention of the party blower. The goal that one might expect the teacher to have in mind is for the child to develop the personal information she has volunteered in response to the story. With such a goal, the outcome certainly cannot be predetermined, nor can the particular procedure adopted be treated as an exemplar of a more general principle (except perhaps of the very vaguely-defined procedure of recounting personal experience fluently). Since the child's experience is personal, the teacher is no more of an authority than the child, and so the relationship should not be that of master and apprentice, but rather that of collaborators. In practice, however, the episode turns into the familiar task of 'guess what's in teacher's mind' – not just once, but twice. It would not be surprising if Stella quickly learned never to offer information unless actually called upon to do so.

What style of interaction, then, would be appropriate for a task of this kind? Put like that, it is difficult to answer without being prescriptive. But one might expect the teacher contribution to take the form of an invitation to continue or a suggestion to focus on a particular aspect of the topic introduced. Questions, if they were used, might be expected to take the form of asking for examples or specific additional detail or of requests for justification of the accuracy or relevance of the contribution – 'How do you know?', 'Why are you telling us this?'

A search through all our recordings yielded only one where episodes of this kind occurred, and it is perhaps significant that it should have been Jacqueline's teacher who provided it. In the following example, she was preparing to read a story about frost, and she wanted to be sure that the children were familiar with the relevant ideas.

T: When I woke up this morning –
I don't know who looked out of the window when they woke up this morning? [Children raise hands]

T: Only – only one two three
Oh four of you
Now who can put their hand up and tell me what they saw out of the window this morning?
Jacquy?

J: Ice

T: Ice
Ice –
Whereabouts was the ice?

				[T waggles her finger]
J:	On the grass			
		T:	On the grass	
J:	On – and on our car			
		T:	That's right It's not. it's .ice – But what do we call it? It's little tiny bits of ice	
C₁:	I call it I call it Jack Frost			
		T:	Frost really, isn't it? Frost What did it make the grass look like?	[T waves hands horizontally in the air]
J:	White			
		T:	White All white? Or was there some green as well?	
C₁:	Some green			
J:	White and green			
		T:	White and green	
C₂:	Mine – Mine was all over the –			
C₃:	The leaves white			
		T:	The leaves were white [To C₃] Yours was all over the [To C₂] grass, was it?	
C₄:	So was mine			
		T:	So was yours?	
Ian:	I had – I had a taste of grass			
		T:	And – Did you?	[T is about to continue then decides to pick up Ian's contribution]

The Complementary Roles of Parents and Teachers   125

	T:	Ian said he had a little taste of it	[T holds up finger to concentrate on Ian's contribution]
		Did it taste of anything?	[To Ian]
J: Yeh			
	T:	What did it taste of?	
J: Taste cold			
	T:	Tastes cold Who knows what ice is? It's something that's frozen	[Pressing fingers of both hands together]
		Ice is made out of something that's frozen	
C$_2$: Well I have that in my drink at home			
J: Cold			
	T:	That's right You have it in your drink at home	[Pointing to C$_2$]
	T:	And how does mummy make it?	
Chn: By water			
	T:	That's right! Ice is WATER that's frozen hard	[Pressing fingers together]
	T:	So that's why it wouldn't really taste very Ian –	[Pointing to Ian who had tasted ice]
		You're right Jacquy It would taste –?	[No answer from J]
		Cold, wouldn't it?	[Touching her lip]
		Cold	
	T:	And you said you had it on your windows Is that right?	[Pointing to J] [J nods]
C: And me			

				[Several other children also speak]
		T:	What did it do on the windows of the car?	
J:	Didn't do nothing			
		T:	It didn't do anything	
C:	You couldn't see out the back window			
J:	No			
		T:	You couldn't see out of the window, no	
J:	It's very dangerous			
J:	Out the back window you couldn't 'cos there is a wire at the back window			
		T:	Oh and it makes – It heats up the back window so the frost disappears?	
J:	Yeh			
		T:	Well then this is a little poem about a man called Mister Jack Frost	[Taking book]
C:	Ooh!			[Children laugh]
		T:	And Mister Jack Frost is the one that comes and creeps down. . And puts all the frost on our windows and on the grass You listen	

The preceding example falls within the content area of knowledge – knowledge about frost and its relation to water. The teacher is drawing upon the children's experience, but she has a clear idea in advance of the facts that should be established before she starts to read the poem. The interaction strategy of asking questions about the children's observations and then generalizing from them seems entirely appropriate, therefore, to the task that she had set, once Jacqueline's first response had been accepted and refined to establish the topic for discussion.

However, to find an example of exploratory talk where the outcome was not determined in advance, I had to turn to a class discussion of *The Pobble who has no Toes* in one of the recordings analysed in Margaret Hocking's study. The teacher's purpose in this case was specifically to encourage the children to make a personal response to the poem, whilst still remaining faithful to the meaning of the text.

T: Shall we just read that bit again?
'His Aunt Jemima
made him drink
Lavender water tinged
with pink.'

C₁: What's lavender water taste like?

T: I don't know
I've never tasted it
Have you?

C₂: We have a drink and it's pink and it's strawberry
And the first time I had it I didn't like it so the next time I put sugar in and I liked it

T: Do you think you would like lavender water?

Chn: No

T: Why not?

C₃: Because when mummy tells me would you like lavender water I says no thank you

T: I wonder why you wouldn't like it though

C: I expect it tastes horrid
C: Nasty
C: Salty

T: You think it would be salty? What do you usually do with lavender water?

C: I don't know I don't know what it is

T: It's a perfume Lavender water is a scent that ladies put on

C: Ugh!

T: It wouldn't be very nice would it to drink?

C: Maybe that's why his toes came off

T: Maybe that did make his toes come off He certainly lost them
T: What about the things he ate? Would you like them? 'Eggs and buttercups fried with fish?'

Chn: No
C: I like the fish and eggs

T: What about the buttercups?

C: I wouldn't like them
C: I don't like fish
C: I don't like flowers and that

T: You don't like flowers Don't you normally eat flowers?

Chn: No

C: Don't you eat cabbage? And cabbage is a flower
C: Yes and you eat cauliflowers
C: You'd not eat flowers that bloom
T: The things that are green
The flowers that are green, yes
C: Can we eat the grass?
Chn: No
C: But the grass is green
T: We don't eat the grass but some animals do
C: The cows eat it
C: Cows
C: Guinea pigs
T: That's right
They like it

    The whole discussion is in this style: the children contributing ideas from their own experience and the teacher helping them to maintain the thread, by picking up the most relevant aspect of each child contribution and using it to extend the exploration. Naturally, there are a number of digressions, such as the discussion of herbivores above, but in the process, as Hocking points out, the children are learning the beginning of the critical method in an interaction which, significantly, is child-initiated and mainly child-sustained.

    It *is* possible, therefore, to develop a style of interaction which is relatively undetermined and open to pupil contributions, yet at the same time appropriate to the chosen task. And because it can embrace spontaneous pupil contributions, it is surely the most effective way of complementing the talk of the home, by building on the foundations that have already been laid in the free-ranging, child-initiated conversations that have been the experience of the vast majority of children before they come to school. At the same time, such talk looks forward to the larger goals of formal education, by introducing the criteria of conformity to experience, internal consistency and relevance, in relation to curricular tasks selected by the teacher.

Since these are the qualities that one would expect teachers to be endeavouring to develop in children's talk, why is it that this style of interaction is so rare in children's first experience of school? A number of explanations might be suggested. The most obvious is that teachers do not, after all, place as much value on these qualities as their public pronouncements would have us believe; at heart they are only concerned to train skills and to drum in facts. However, I do not believe that this is, in fact, the case. More probable, it seems, is that they do value such qualities but in a rather diffuse way that does not fully inform their moment-by-moment interactions in the classroom. Other pressures, such as the desire to be seen to be efficient, and to keep to a well-prepared programme of work, take on a greater priority, and control of the class – or the loss of control that is feared if children are allowed to take the initiative in task-related talk – assumes an overriding importance. It is certainly true that a high proportion of children's spontaneous contributions to class or group discussion are in varying degrees irrelevant to the immediate task, and 30 or more children all wanting to develop their own line of thought pose a serious threat to the teacher's control over discussion. But before we accept this explanation at face value, we should stop to ask 'Irrelevant to whom?' Not to the children, presumably, since they are prepared to speak out in front of their peers, and struggle to make their meaning clear. The irrelevance must, therefore, be in the mind of the teacher, who has planned in advance the course that the children's learning should take. But what is relevant to the teacher may be irrelevant to the children, unless they are helped to relate their personal experiences to the task in hand, and teacher control may be bought at the expense of the full and active involvement of the children.

Relevance in talk is only a particular case of matching means to ends, procedures to goals, and in many spheres of activity children have already achieved considerable competence of this sort, particularly where the goal is self-chosen. What makes talk a special case, however, is that it is a reciprocal activity, in which both participants have to be prepared to negotiate their meanings towards the attainment of a shared goal. Relevance in talk is thus essentially a matter for negotiation. But it is through such negotiation of meaning that language is first acquired, with parents helping children to match utterances to the understanding they both have of a shared situation. By the time they come to school, children already have some understanding of relevance in talk, as can be seen in the conversations that they themselves initiate. What schools should provide, therefore, is the opportunity to develop and extend these conversational skills by putting them to use in the exploration of the new ideas and experiences that the more formal curriculum provides. However, this is only possible if at least some curricular tasks adopt a style of interaction which is truly reciprocal, and where the goal of the task is sufficiently open-ended for the relevance of the children's contributions to be negotiated as the talk proceeds. Only in this way will children develop the confidence and skill to use talk as a means of understanding and controlling the world in which they live. Our problem as teachers is to learn how to maintain the supportive responsiveness of parents, whilst at the same time complementing it with a clear sense of the skills and knowledge that we wish to make available.

CHAPTER 7
Story Reading and the Development of Symbolic Skills

In Chapter 5, I reported some of the main findings from the study in which we followed 32 of the children through the first two years of school. The aim of the study, as the title of the chapter suggested, was to find out what factors contributed most to success in the early years of schooling and, given the preoccupation of many educators at the time when the study was planned with the notion of 'linguistic disadvantage', we looked very closely at linguistic differences between children at the point of entry to school. We certainly found such differences but, as far as oral language was concerned, they appeared to be of degree rather than of kind: all children seemed to be following the same general pattern of development only some were making more rapid progress than others. We were further able to show that, to a considerable extent, children's rate of language learning was affected by the quality of the conversation that they experienced with their parents and other members of their immediate community. However, since differences in rate of development and in quality of conversational experience were not significantly related to family background (Barnes et al., 1983), it was clearly not here that an explanation would be found of the relationship between social class and educational attainment.

On the other hand there was another kind of difference between the children that we had observed that did seem to be potentially more explanatory, and that was the extent of their knowledge of literacy on entry to school. This we found to be a powerful predictor of later attainment both at seven years and again when we assessed the children at 10+. It was also significantly related to family background. The question that was not answered by this study, however, concerned the precise nature of the pre-school experiences that led some children to score much more highly on the test of knowledge of literacy than others. It was to answer this question that the investigation reported here was addressed.

The tests we used (Clay, 1972b) measured certain aspects of children's skills in dealing with the graphic properties of print – the layout of a book, the left-to-right, top-to-bottom conventions of writing and the names or sounds of letters. It might seem, therefore, that it was possession of this knowledge that accounted for the relatively rapid progress in learning to read and write that characterized high scorers on the test. However I do not think that this is the case. Certainly, in becoming literate, one does acquire and use this knowledge, but reading and writing also involve a great deal more than mastery of the 'mechanics' of written language. More probable, it seemed to me, was that the knowledge about the mechanics of literacy that some children have on entry to school is a relatively superficial by-product of a much more fundamental understanding of the essential characteristics of written language that they have gained from their experience of written language in use in their own homes.

To find out more about possibly relevant pre-school experiences I searched through the transcripts of all the recordings of spontaneous conversation for any occurrence of activities that might be considered to be related to reading and writing. These activities were grouped into four categories: looking at books or magazines; listening to a story read aloud; drawing and colouring; writing or pretending to write. The last category occurred so rarely that it subsequently had to be omitted from the analysis. For all the rest, frequency scores were computed for each child and these were compared with three of the language measures obtained at school: Knowledge about Literacy on entry to school; Reading Comprehension at seven years and the Oral Language section of the Teacher Assessment at five. The results were absolutely clear cut. Of the various pre-school activities related to reading, only listening to stories was significantly associated with later language measures and it was associated with all three of them.*

What's in a Story?

Why should listening to stories be so much more beneficial than looking at books and talking about the pictures or learning to represent ideas graphically through drawing and colouring? The answer, I believe, lies in the particular relationship between language and experience that is found in stories – and in most extended used of written language.

In ordinary conversation, the meanings that are communicated arise out of the context of present activity or out of past or future events about which the participants have shared knowledge or

---

*Fuller details can be found in Wells (1985b).

expectations. To understand what is meant, therefore, they can use the context to help them interpret what is said. In the case of written language, by contrast, writer and reader do not usually know what knowledge they share and there is no context independent of the written text itself. Thus, whereas in spoken language meanings are supported by the context in which they occur, in written language it is the text which provides the only evidence from the sender to enable the receiver to *create* the context to understand the meanings of which the text consists. Understanding a story, therefore – or any other written text – requires one to pay particularly careful attention to the language in order to build up the structure of meaning, for this is conveyed to the reader by the words and structures alone (Olson, 1977).

In listening to stories read aloud at the age of two or three or four – long before they can read themselves – children are thus beginning to gain experience of the sustained meaning-building organization of written language and of its characteristic rhythms and structures. They are also learning to pay attention to the linguistic message as the major source of meaning for, even when the book is illustrated, the story requires no other context than itself for its interpretation. 'There once was an old man who lived in a little thatched cottage at the edge of a dark and mysterious forest . . .' But, most importantly, the child is beginning to come to grips with the symbolic potential of language – its power to represent experience in symbols which are independent of the objects, events and relationships which are symbolized, and which can be interpreted in contexts other than those in which the experience originally occurred.

Learning to recognize their own names in writing, or to write them themselves or matching names or sounds to the letters of the alphabet, by contrast, although useful, are of much less importance. The same is true of the learning that takes place when looking at picture books and magazines and discussing the names and attributes of the objects depicted. No doubt this helps children to enlarge their vocabulary – at least for those things that can be pictured; it also gives them practice in answering display questions of a limited kind. This may well give them an initial advantage if they find themselves – as so many children do – in classrooms where such skills are emphasized. But it is a short-lived advantage and one which is, in the longer term, restricting. For ultimately, and ideally sooner rather than later, they will need to be able to answer – and to ask – questions that go beyond naming. They will need to follow and construct narrative and expository sequences, recognize causes, anticipate consequences and consider the motives and emotions that are inextricably bound up with all human actions and endeavours.

Story Reading and the Development of Symbolic Skills 135

For this, the experience of stories is probably the ideal preparation. At first, of course, the stories that children have read to them will be of most value to them in extending their experience vicariously and in encouraging and providing validation for their own inner storying (Spencer, 1976) – what has been called 'the fictionalizing of self' (Scollon and Scollon, 1981). Gradually, however, they will lead them to reflect on their experience and, in so doing, to discover the power that language has, through its symbolic potential, to create and explore alternative possible worlds with their own inner coherence and logic. Stories may thus lead to the imaginative, hypothetical stance that is required in a wide range of intellectual activities and for problem-solving of all kinds.

However, such results are not inevitable. Reading stories to children *may* help them to develop these sorts of control over language, but a great deal will depend on the sort of stories that are read and on the talk that accompanies or follows their reading. Whether they be concerned with familiar everyday events or with the experiences of more remote, or imagined people and creatures, the stories must be written in a way which grips the child's imagination. Discussion of them, too, should not be restricted to a checking of facts and recall of detail for its own sake, but should encourage children to explore the world created through the language of the book and to relate it to their own experience.

This can be seen happening in the following extract from a recording of David (aged three years), who has chosen *The Giant Jam Sandwich* (Lord and Burroway, 1974) for his mother to read to him. Notice how the mother leaves space for the child to offer his comments and how her contributions build on his, extending his understanding of both the matter of the story and the actual wording.

M: 'One hot summer in Itching Down   [M reads]
Four million wasps flew into town'
D: I don't like wasps. . . . flying into town
M: Why's that?
D: Because they sting me
M: Do they?
D: Mm. I don't like them

		M:	They'll only sting you if they get angry If you leave them alone they won't sting you But four million would be rather a lot wouldn't it? They'd get rather in the way 'They drove the picknickers away' [M reads]
D:	Mm		
		M:	'They chased the farmers from their hay They stung Lord Swell (chuckles) on his fat bald' –
D:	Pate		
		M:	D'you know what a pate is?
D:	What?		
		M:	What d'you think it is?
D:	Hair		
		M:	Well – yes
		M:	It's where his hair SHOULD be It's his head – look his BALD head All his hair's gone
D:	Where is it?		
		M:	Well he's old so it's dropped out He's gone bald
D:	Where's – Is that his hat?		
		M:	Mm . . He's running so his hat is falling off . . 'They dived.and hummed.and buzzed.and ate' [M reads]
D:	D'they eat him?		
		M:	(laughs) I expect they might have tried to [M turns page] I dunno D'you think wasps eat people?
D:	No		
		M:	What do they eat?
D:	They eat vegetables		
		M:	Vegetables (laughing)
D:	Yes		
		M:	What sort? What do they like?

D: They like . . .
Um . . .

M: What kind of vegetables were you thinking of?

D: Is that a spray to shoo them away?
Is that a spray to shoo them away?

M: Yes it's probably some sort of insecticide.to get rid of them
And what's that net for do you think?

D: It's for catching them with

M: It doesn't seem to be much good though does it?

D: No they come out the holes

M: (laughs) The holes are too big aren't they?
And what about this man? [M points to man
What's he got? in picture who is wielding a fly swat]

D: He's –
What's he got?

M: What's that?

D: A note
What does the note say?

M: A note on a stick is it?
Is that what you think?

D: Actually it's a sound

M: A what?

D: A sound
What's it called on the – on the stick?
What is that on –
What's that man got?

M: Well you know um –

D: Yes . .
Sign

M: You think it's a sign
Yes it looks very like a sign with writing on doesn't it?

D:	Yes		
		M:	But it isn't It's like Mummy's – um – fish slice
D:	What is it?		
		M:	It's a swatter He's going to hit the wasp with it
D:	How d'you hit wasps watters?		
		M:	Swatters? (checking) Well they're made of plastic usually
D:	Yes		
		M:	And they – you bang them down See if you can squash the wasp . . Looks very angry
D:	Is he going to sting him?		
		M:	Maybe he's already been stung That's why he's so cross . . 5 . .
D:	Is he hurt?		
		M:	It looks as if he might be He's making a funny face
D:	Why he making a funny face? Is that man – Is that man shouting for them to go away?		
		M:	Think so He's got his mouth open so he could be shouting . . . Anyway –
D:	Yes		
		M:	'They called a meeting. in the village hall [M reads] And Mayor Muddlenut asked them all "What can we do?" And they said. "Good question!" But nobody had a good suggestion Then Bap the Baker leaped to his feet And cried. "What do wasps like. <u>best</u> to –

D: Best
   Eat
                    M: Strawberry –
D: Jam
                    M: Now wait a minute
                       If we made a giant SANDWICH
D: Yes
                    M: We could trap them in it'

Conversation of this kind requires a light touch, a willingness to listen and to follow the child's lead, helping him to develop and clarify his own interpretation, rather than imposing one that is 'correct' – from an adult point of view. But, of course, these qualities are desirable, whenever possible, in all interactions between adults and children, not just when reading stories. For, whether at home or at school, the child learns most effectively when meanings are negotiated within a relationship marked by reciprocity.

Conclusion

I started this chapter by describing how we have attempted to identify which aspects of early linguistic experience are associated with attainment in the early stages of schooling and I have reported results which support the widely accepted belief that reading stories to children is particularly beneficial. It is so partly because hearing stories read aloud familiarizes them with the language of books and with the characteristic narrative structures that they will meet in story books at school. It may also have the useful side-effect of introducing them to some of the 'mechanical' aspects of reading and writing. But most importantly, I have argued, hearing stories introduces children to language being used in a way which is independent of any context other than that created by the language itself.

The ability to deal with 'disembedded' language, to pay attention to the meaning carried by the verbal message, without looking for support from or being distracted by the immediate context, is one which is of particular importance in school, as so much of the experience that makes up the school curriculum can only be encountered in the classroom in symbolic form – in the spoken words of the teacher and in textbooks and works of reference. As Margaret Donaldson puts it:

What is going to be required for success in our educational system is that [the child] should learn to turn language and thought in upon themselves. He must become able to direct his own thought processes in a thoughtful manner. He must become able not just to talk, but to choose what he will say, not just to interpret but to weigh possible interpretations. His conceptual system must expand in the direction of increasing ability to represent itself. He must become capable of manipulating symbols (1978, pp.88–9).

Stories read aloud and discussed in a way which encourages reflection upon their own experience and imaginative exploration of the world created through the language of the text are probably the best way of helping young children to begin to develop these abilities. If this argument is correct, we should be all the more ready to meet the request, 'Please will you read me a story?'

CHAPTER 8
The Relevance of Applied Linguistics for Teachers of Reading

The ability to read and write one's native language is one of the prime aims of education, and teachers rightly look for all the help they can find to enable them to ensure the success of each child. In recent years, as emphasis has refocused on the essentially linguistic basis of reading and writing, increasing attention has been paid to theoretical work in linguistics and the related disciplines of psycholinguistics and sociolinguistics, and a number of books have appeared under titles such as *Linguistics and Reading,* which offer a theoretical perspective on the teaching of reading and writing drawn from these disciplines.

However, whilst not wishing to cast doubt on the value, for teachers of reading, of serious study of language, we wish in this chapter to treat the relevance of such study as problematic, and to investigate the ways in which the theories about language developed by linguists, psycholinguists and sociolinguists are actually felt to be helpful by those concerned with teaching children to read. The authors are both involved in the further education of teachers, so one natural line of investigation was to talk with a number of teachers of reading who have recently been engaged in full- or part-time study, and whose courses have included various aspects of applied linguistics, in order to discover what they had gained from their studies. An observational study of children learning to read that we are conducting provided another perspective on the question, and in the second part of the chapter we shall consider the extent to which linguistic theory assists in the interpretation of the data that have been collected.

First of all let us consider the teachers, all of whom have been engaged in study for post-experience higher awards in the School of Education at the University of Bristol. We first asked them how the knowledge of linguistics and related subjects that they had gained had affected their teaching of reading. In every case the answer was positive, and they mentioned a number of specific changes they had made in their teaching as a result of their studies.

Mrs. Clifford, for example, who is deputy head of a junior school (age range 7–11 years), explained how her study had brought about 'a shift in emphasis from decoding words sequentially, to showing children how they can utilise the central skills of reading, even when they are novices', and she explained how she now 'encourages children, on meeting an unknown word, to read on to the end of the phrase or sentence and "guess" the missing word from the context'.

Mr Peabody, who is a remedial teacher working with children aged between 8 and 13 years, stressed the completely new approach he now takes to hearing children read – a time-honoured custom in British schools. Whereas in the past he 'had seen this activity as providing children with an opportunity for practising their skills', he now considers it to have 'a very important diagnostic function in allowing him to identify the strategies that the children are using'. He, like most of the other teachers we talked to, is making use of a modified version of the 'mis-cue inventory' (Goodman and Burke, 1972) to analyse errors in reading aloud, in order to gain greater understanding of individual children's strengths and weaknesses.

Miss Hareclive, who teaches the youngest age children (5–7 years), described how she had been led to a much more careful consideration of the similarities and differences between spoken and written language. This had helped her to see more clearly how to use a 'language experience' approach, building on the children's existing expertise in oral language. She had also become more aware of the ways in which differences between spoken and written language might cause problems, such as, for example, the different purposes for which the two media are typically used and the apparent dissimilarity between 'the continuous flow of speech' and the way in which a written message 'is broken up into units with spaces in between'.

Helping children to grasp the connection between the language they confidently use when talking and listening and the initially strange visual array presented by a written or printed text is central to a language experience approach and some children need considerable assistance in making this connection. As Marie Clay points out:

> a child may have developed good visual perception for forms and shapes and yet fail to learn to read because he thinks the task depends on visual memory for particular letters or forms and does not appreciate that his power to produce language has anything to do with it. Similarly a child with good language skills may be unsuccessful in applying these to reading because

The Relevance of Applied Linguistics for Teachers of Reading

he does not pay the visual cues sufficient attention (Clay, 1972a, p.6).

From these and other comments, there was no doubt that this group of teachers had gained much of practical significance from their studies. Taking all their answers together, a general picture emerged of what they now see to be the main considerations in helping children learn to read. They can be summarized as follows:

1. Getting meaning from print
    (a) Emphasis, first and foremost, on making sense of written language; using expectations derived from the text, both preceding and following, as well as from personal experience, to overcome the barriers presented by unknown or difficult words;
    (b) Importance of maintaining an appropriate balance between 'predicting' and 'decoding' skills;
    (c) Using children's 'errors' when reading aloud to diagnose problems.
2. Relationship between spoken and written language
    (a) Preference for working from larger units to smaller units when teaching analysis of both spoken and written language: making comparisons between whole messages first, then words and morphemes, before teaching relationships between phonemes or phoneme clusters and graphemes and grapheme clusters;
    (b) Awareness of the importance of using written material that draws upon the sort of spoken language that children are familiar with – at least in the early stages;
    (c) Recognition that a written text can be read aloud just as easily in an accent, and that speakers of non-standard dialects need not be handicapped if different forms are recognized as equivalent in meaning.
3. Purposes for reading and writing
    (a) Emphasis on finding genuine purposes for reading and writing, and on developing appropriate strategies for different purposes;
    (b) Initial emphasis on enjoyment of reading; listening to stories being read loud.

Perhaps the most important characteristic of this group of teachers is their emphasis on helping children to build up and maintain *meaning momentum*: in their teaching they now see that training in specific skills to do with letter identification and letter and sound matching, important though these are, must be subordinated to the larger aim of encouraging children to acquire a wide range of useful strategies for discovering a writer's message. On the basis of these answers, the relevance of linguistic studies might seem to have been established beyond doubt. However, when we asked these same teachers which particular aspects of linguistics they found most helpful, they were less certain. Clearly, it was not the specific content of any particular grammatical description such as is presented, for example, in various Transformational–Generative grammars of English. Nor were even the basic principles of the theory – notions of generative and transformational rules, or the distinction between competence and performance – felt to be particularly relevant. Even in the associated disciplines of psycholinguistics and sociolinguistics, they found it quite difficult to pick out writers or researchers whose work was immediately relevant. In fact, what these teachers had absorbed during the course of their studies, it appeared, was not so much applicable theories, as a deepened interest in language as a human phenomenon, and a greater willingness to stand back and consider afresh what it means to communicate through language. As a result, they had arrived at new insights about how children can be helped to acquire skill, confidence and satisfaction through using and developing their communicative abilities.

The description that one of the group gave of linguistics as 'the study of language in a *communication* context, where a great deal of attention is paid to intended and expressed *meaning,* and not just to what appears on the surface' (speaker's emphases) serves to underline this point. This is more a description of what, from his point of view as a teacher, he felt linguistic studies ought to be about, than about the actual content of most theoretical work in linguistic or related disciplines, at the present time. Indeed, when one looks back at the contributions that eminent linguists have made to the debate on reading during the last 20 years, the topics that they seem to have been *least* concerned with are 'communication' and 'meaning'.

In interpreting the teachers' replies in this way, we do not wish to denigrate the very proper concerns of linguists, nor to suggest that the teachers had failed to understand the significance of linguistic studies, but rather to suggest some doubts about the current vogue for the wholesale incorporation of linguistic theory into the very different domain of planning curriculum activities, and of carrying out those plans – even when these curriculum activities are linguistic. Our point is that the concerns of linguists and teachers are different, and this will be reflected in the way in which they think about language and language behaviour. Real children do not conform to idealized models constructed by the theorists, nor are the problems that the children encounter, and which teachers have to deal with, necessarily those to which the linguists have given their attention.

This is probably nowhere more true than in the very early stages of learning to read, which is the subject of the observational research referred to above. The 20 children being studied were selected from a much larger sample, whose pre-school language development has been monitored since 1973 in a longitudinal study being carried out at the University of Bristol. One of the aims of the study is to investigate the ways in which children draw upon the skills they already have as native speakers and listeners when they start to learn to use the written form of language.

The implication of much recent psycholinguistic research on reading is that the main difference between reading and listening lies in the different sensory modalities employed, and that what the beginning reader chiefly has to learn, therefore, is the correspondence between the two systems of representation. Hence the emphasis on reading for meaning, since it is assumed that, by concentrating on the level at which spoken and written messages are most similar, strategies developed for coping with spoken messages will help beginning readers to use cues that are already available to them and allow them to gain the 'meaning momentum' which is essential for effective reading at any level.

Although we were in broad agreement with those theorists who emphasize the general similarity between reading and listening, we were nevertheless aware of important differences between the two activities, as they are encountered by young children, which require many children who have successfully mastered the systems of spoken language to spend quite a period of time being initiated into the activity of reading. We are referring here not simply to the learning of phoneme–grapheme correspondences and the spatial conventions of writing, important though these are. Even more fundamental for initial progress, we believe, in an understanding of the purposes of reading and writing, and of the fact that messages can be sent and received through solitary and silent interaction with marks on paper, as well as through face-to-face speech encounters with other people. Children also vary considerably in their initial motivation for the task of learning to read, as a result of their pre-school experience at home; there are, in addition, large differences in the circumstances of their first encounters with the printed word either at home or in the more formal context of the classroom. All these factors seem likely to have an influence on the success with which children change from being non-readers to being able to read with confidence and fluency, and the aim of the research is to attempt to gain a better understanding of the complex processes involved.

One way of doing this is by observing the progress of individual children, and this is what we have been doing, through regular visits to the schools of the 20 children involved. In addition to administering appropriate tests of reading attainment at the beginning and end of the school year, we have made written and video records of the moment-by-moment activities of these children over the course of a complete morning once every month.

The teachers of all these children are using what might be generally described as a 'language experience' approach, and they try as far as possible to arrange individual or small group activities that are appropriate to the needs of these children, as they perceive them. However, one of the things that very quickly emerged from our observations was how little we, as teachers, know about how *the children* perceive the tasks that are traditionally set for them at this stage. Consider the following examples:

> Paul (age 5 years) has just started school. He has drawn a picture of himself, riding his bicycle in the park, and his teacher has written a caption to his dictation. He sits at his table, copying under the teacher's writing, working more or less systematically from bottom right to top left in forming both words and letters. When he runs out of space, he fits the remaining words in wherever there is a space in his drawing.
>
> Wendy (5 years 4 months) and a friend have been given a reading game to play, in which they are required to match words and pictures. Having explained the game to them, their teacher leaves them to play by themselves, but after a few rather unsuccessful attempts, the two girls find an alternative use for the cards as they play shops, with the cards as money.
>
> Philip (5 years 3 months) is invited to read to his teacher from Dick Bruna's book *I Can Read*. As can be seen from the transcript of this session, he knows enough about what reading involves to justify his version by pointing, correctly, to specify letters. But at a more fundamental level he has almost no idea at all about how these letters convey the precise meaning of the text

Text	*Philip*	*Teacher*
This is my nose	Girl	Why do you say 'girl'?

	It's got an 'e'e on the front	
	(points to the 'e' in 'nose')	
and this is my mouth	Girl	How do you know it's 'girl'
	'Cos it's got a 'd' on the end	
	(points to 'd' in 'and')	
This is my front	Girl	
and this is my back	Girl	Is it?
	'Cos it's got that on the end	
	a 'd' (points to 'd' in 'and')	

The problems illustrated by Philip, Wendy and Paul – and many others like them – are not caused by culturally irrelevant material nor by lack of ability in the spoken language; nor are they likely to be overcome by emphasizing the use of context cues, or by careful training with a structured programme of phonics, useful though both these approaches may be at a later stage. Before they can begin the make real progress in reading, they will somehow have to discover for themselves that written language can have meaning for *them*, and that this meaning is systematically related to the particular visual array of marks on the page, in a very similar way to that in which they understand the meaning of what is said to them from the particular sequence of sounds that is spoken.

Fortunately, however, most children *do* make this discovery and, as some of our observations from the end of the first year at school show, they develop their own strategies for dealing with the systematic relationship of meaning to print.

Wendy, for example, at six years has learnt to write her own simple stories and has developed for herself the helpful strategy of taking her writing 'on the run'. Whenever she stops writing to talk to her friends – which occurs after almost every word – she forgets where she has got to in composing her sentence. Each time this happens, however, she goes back to the beginning of the sentence and reads and matches each word until she reaches the point where she broke off, and in this way she regains the momentum to continue with her writing.

James is another child who has made the break-through during the year. Aged 5 years 9 months and reading aloud to his teacher, he breaks off to talk about the words:

James: (reads) As they walk up the hill they see a fireman they. . .know-

(comments) I keep getting it wrong because it's got a 'k' on the end
Teacher: Yes it's difficult isn't it?
James: And it – without the 'k' it says 'now' and without that and that (pointing to 'k' and 'w') it says 'no'. . .difficult!
Teacher: Yes I know. But you know it. You got it right didn't you?

This short episode is interesting in showing the awareness that James has of the structure of written language, and of the way in which differences in meaning are related to specific arrangements of letters. However, the question to which we are still seeking an answer is *how* children like Wendy and James make their individual discoveries. For it is only when we understand this that we shall be able to plan for it to happen, rather than simply wait and hope.

Some suggestions can be gleaned from linguistic research, but by no means a conclusive answer. For example, research on language acquisition in recent years has begun to emphasize the importance of the situationally relevant utterances that are addressed to young children by their parents and other adults, in providing an opportunity for them to discover the relationship between the functions and meanings that are intended and the actual selection and arrangement of linguistic elements in these spoken utterances. It can be assumed, therefore, that similar presentations of relevant written messages will be helpful for the discovery of the relationship between meaning and written language. But the parallel is not complete, as the need to acquire control of spoken language is far more compelling than the need felt by many children to acquire an additional medium of communication, even when they have realized that writing does indeed have a communicative function.

Ensuring the similarity between the written language children encounter in school and the spoken language they are using both in and out of school has also been suggested as theoretically likely to help them see the connection, and this is central, of course, to the 'language experience' approach. Certainly, practices such as writing down the stories that children tell so they are able to read texts of their own composition provide opportunities for making the connection, but the opportunities are not always grasped.

Playing with the forms of spoken language, through puns, nonsense rhymes and so on, has also been suggested as a help in learning to read, since grasping the rather abstract connection between meaning, speech and the spatial arrangement of word and letters in writing, requires the learner to treat 'language forms as

The Relevance of Applied Linguistics for Teachers of Reading

opaque and attend to them in and for themselves' (Cazden, 1973, p.3). Certainly, pleasure and interest in manipulating language forms has been associated with success in the case of James, whose comments on the spelling of 'know' were quoted above. James is making excellent progress.

But how do these theoretical suggestions help to explain the relative lack of progress made by Philip, who, at the end of the first year, is still only at the stage of talking about the pictures in his books. Philip comes from a well-educated family where there is ample evidence of the importance of reading. His parents frequently read stories to him and take him on visits to museums, both of which activities Philip enjoys very much. At school he has many friends and he is a very successful conversationalist. He also has a clear grasp of the social importance of being able to read: challenged on one occasion by another child who disbelieved his claim to be able to read, Philip picked up a book that neither he nor the other child was able to read, and gave a very convincing performance of 'reading' the story aloud. Nevertheless, he has not yet discovered the actual relationship between language and print.

From one point of view, these particular children can be seen, along with many others, as providing evidence for or against particular theories, and that is a perfectly proper point of view for the linguist or psycholinguist to take. From another point of view, however, they illustrate the sort of everyday experience that teachers have to understand as best they can, so that they can plan their classroom programmes. The question is: what should be the relationship between these points of view? Should teachers see their role as that of assimilating the theories provided by the linguists, psychologists and other researchers, in order to apply them in their teaching? Or is there some other, less dependent, way of conceiving the relationship?

We believe that there is, and that it has already been indicated by the teachers whose views we quoted above. These teachers had, very wisely, not attempted directly to absorb and apply the linguistic theory that they had met in their courses, for they had not found it to be particularly relevant. Instead, they had started to construct their own theories of reading and learning to read, and some of their ideas had been suggested to them by the study of language that they had engaged in. However, it was noticeable that the writers whose work they had found particularly helpful were such people as Kenneth and Yetta Goodman, Frank Smith and Courtney Cazden, whom they had perceived to be less linguists or psycholinguists, than educators with aims similar to their own.

This, in our opinion, is entirely appropriate. In the first place, as we have already seen, linguistic theory has not concerned itself with all the problems about which teachers have to make decisions, nor is there agreement amongst linguists on quite fundamental issues such as the importance of teaching phoneme–grapheme correspondences, and the form that such teaching should take. As Noam Chomsky himself has said 'I am frankly rather sceptical about the significance, for the teaching of language, of such insights as have been attained in linguistics and psychology . . . It is difficult to believe that either linguistics or psychology has achieved a level of theoretical understanding that might enable it to support a "technology" of language teaching' (Chomsky, 1966). More recently, Courtney Cazden (1976) has suggested similar reservations in an article entitled 'How knowledge about language helps the classroom teacher – or does it?'

Secondly, and more importantly, the aims of linguists and teachers are essentially different. Linguistics is a descriptive science, whereas teaching is, in the positive sense of the term, a prescriptive art. This is not to suggest that linguists take no interest in the applications of the theories that they construct on the basis of empirical observations, nor that teachers will not make more effective decisions as a result of acquiring an understanding of the linguists' theories. But, as Cazden (*op. cit.*) suggests, if the theoretical knowledge is to be helpful, it must be carefully selected and restructured into an action-oriented programme. Which is to suggest that teachers should be theory constructors too, but constructors of theories that relate directly to their classroom practice.

An analogy may help to clarify the distinction. There is a very respectable branch of accoustical research which is concerned to describe and account for the characteristic sounds produced by the different instruments of the orchestra. It seems reasonable to assume that knowledge derived from such study would be interesting, and perhaps even helpful, to the aspiring composer. But if he is to achieve the symphonic effect that he has in mind, we should hardly advise him to treat composition as the application of this branch of accoustical physics. Rather, we should advise him to look to the theory of orchestration for assistance and, in time, we might expect the successful composer to contribute to the theory through his own unique creative ability. In the course of this, the composer may make use of information derived from accoustical physics, but only in so far as it helps him to achieve the musical effect he is striving towards.

Of course, the analogy must not be pressed too far. Nevertheless, our contention is that teachers are more akin to composers than to research physicists, and that the sort of theories that they will find helpful are those that are developed and refined in relation to their own creative experience of working with children.

The relevance of linguistic theory, therefore, is a matter for each individual teacher to decide. In attempting to construct useful theoretical frameworks to guide the decisions they must make in planning appropriate learning experiences for the different children in their classes, teachers will want to build bridges out towards a wide variety of sources of information and explanation, including the linguistic sciences. But they will also want to test the value of the ideas they bring back against the practical criterion: do they help me to teach more effectively and to understand why some courses of action are more successful than others? Only where this criterion is met, will the ideas justify the carriage.

In conclusion, we should like to quote again from Noam Chomsky (1966), for who better than a linguist can urge the case for the teachers to decide for themselves on the relevance of linguistics to the teaching of reading:

> Teachers have a responsibility to make sure that ideas and proposals are evaluated on their merits, and not passively accepted on grounds of authority, real or presumed. The field of language teaching is no exception. It is possible – even likely – that principles of psychology and linguistics, and research in these disciplines, may supply insights useful to the language teacher. But this must be demonstrated, and cannot be presumed. It is the language teacher himself who must validate or refute any specific proposal. There is very little in psychology or linguistics that he can accept on faith.

CHAPTER 9
Language, Learning and the Curriculum

How do children learn to talk and how do they, in talking, learn about other things? What kinds of talk with other people, particularly their parents and teachers, help them to learn most effectively? These are some of the questions that we have been trying to answer during the last decade as we have followed a group of Bristol children, observing and recording them in their homes and later in their classrooms. In this chapter I shall be concerned chiefly with the contribution that adults can make to children's learning through their conversations with them.

On average, about three utterances a minute are addressed to children by adults, hour after hour, day after day, week after week, both at home and at school. What is said and the purpose in saying it varies enormously from utterance to utterance, depending upon the specific context in which it occurs. Probably very few individual utterances are of any long-term significance but, over a period of time, the relative frequency of different kinds of utterance spoken by any one adult begins to constitute a recognizable style, and different styles convey quite different messages to children about who they are and how they are expected to behave.

Of particular importance are the kinds of message that concern the value that is placed upon their attempts to make sense of their experience – of their active exploration of their environment and of their interpretation of the consequences of their own and other people's actions. From such messages – the 'hidden curriculum', as it has been called – children internalize images of themselves as learners, and of their abilities to recognize and solve problems for themselves.

These self-images are, I believe, of very considerable consequence, not only for their learning in school, but also for the quality of their life after they leave school and for the sort of contribution that they are able to make to the wider society of which they are growing up to be members. Because this is so, it is essential, in my opinion, that we, parents and teachers, should look very carefully at the styles we adopt when interacting with the children for whom we are responsible.

The purpose of this chapter, then, is to draw upon observations of children at home and at school in order to consider the messages conveyed by different styles of adult–child interaction and, on this basis, to make certain suggestions concerning the organization of the curriculum.

Children's Early Learning

The first phase of our study was concerned with the early years and involved a representative sample of 128 children. From 15 months onwards we used radio-microphones to obtain samples of the children's interaction with those in their immediate home surroundings – parents, brothers and sisters and relatives and friends of the family. By means of a pre-set timing device we were able to avoid the inhibiting effect of a researcher in the home and thus to obtain recordings of spontaneously occurring conversation from the wide range of contexts that make up everyday life at home.

As we analysed these recordings, we noticed particularly how actively children engage in learning. There is no curriculum and little that is recognizable as direct teaching, yet all the children we observed made great progress in learning their native language and simultaneously in learning, through language, about the world in which they lived. All were noticing features of interest and asking questions about them, meeting problems and trying to find solutions to them, sometimes on their own, sometimes by enlisting adult assistance. There were no non-verbal children, none who were not active makers of meaning.

Equally evident was the part played by the parents and other adults who interacted with the children. Although rarely engaging in direct teaching, their influence on their children's development was to be seen in the model of mature behaviour that they provided and in their sustaining, through rewarding interaction, of their children's motivation to learn. For a high proportion of the time they treated the children as equal partners in conversation, encouraging them to take the initiative and helping them to extend the topics that they proposed. There were, of course, differences between homes in this respect but, generally speaking, most children experienced a reciprocal form of interaction, in which meanings were negotiated, not unilaterally imposed.

This style of interaction is well illustrated in the excerpt from the recording of James, made when he was aged 3½ years. Mother is concerned to see that James changes his muddy clothes after he has been in the garden, but, when he draws her attention to a bird that he can see, she sets her concern on one side for a moment in order to share his interest and to extend it by explaining the bird's behaviour.

M: There we are
There – one slipper on

J: I can see a bird

M: A what, love?

J: See a bird

M: Is there? Outside? [M whispers]

J: Yes [J also whispers]
See [He points to the bird]

M: Is he eating anything? [Whispering continues by both]

J: No

M: Where?
Oh yes, he's getting –
Do you know what he's doing?

J: No

M: He's going to the ..
the .. paper sack to
try and pick out some
pieces –
Oh, he's got some
food there
And I expect he'll
pick out some pieces
of thread from the
sack to go and make
his nest .. up ..
underneath the
roof, James
Wait a minute and I'll – [J now wants to go out to see]
OK wait a mo – wait a
mo James

J: That bird's gone

M: Has it gone now? [Normal speech volume]

J: Yes

    M: Oh
    Take those long
    trousers off because
    they're a bit muddy in
    in there.
    One...oops...ooh   [Getting J out of
                              his trousers]
    There (laughs)
    One sock on and one
    sock off   [One sock has
                           come off with
                           the trousers]

J: Yes

    M: One sock –   [Utterance is cut
                           off by J]

J: I want s–
   I want s–
   I only want one
   sock on

    M: Come on
    You'll have your sock
    on properly please

In claiming that, except in relation to such matters as safety and acceptable behaviour, most parents do not deliberately teach their children, I do not wish to suggest that they do not provide opportunities for them to learn, nor that they are not sometimes conscious of so doing. The point is, rather that, in such 'extending' conversations as this between James and his mother, the information that is offered to the child, and from which he may learn if he chooses, arises quite spontaneously in response to the child's expression of interest and is a natural outcome of the adult's desire to share in the child's interest or activity. It is also worth noting that the language of the mother's explanation is relatively complex but, because he is actively interested in the topic, James is strongly motivated to try to understand what is said. So he is learning language at the same time as he is using language to learn other things.

    An important characteristic of much of children's learning at home is that it occurs in the context of purposeful practical activity, often jointly engaged in with an adult. Although the skills and knowledge that they acquire may be more or less tied to the immediate context, they are likely to be effectively learned because they are a means to a goal of their own choosing. At the same time, they are gaining confidence in their own ability to formulate problems and deploy strategies for finding solutions.

However, for the majority of children, the horizon of learning is not limited to the here and now. Recalling past events and making plans for the future provide opportunities to gain a broader perspective. For the more fortunate, there is also the experience of listening to stories read aloud, which introduces them to the power that language, especially written language, has to create 'alternative possible worlds' to be explored through the imagination. The conversation that arises from stories, if it is open-ended and exploratory, is particularly rich in opportunities for children to make connections and comparisons between aspects of their experience and, thereby, to begin to develop a more reflective and consciously inquiring attitude to their experience.

From Home to First School

By the time children come to school at five, therefore, they have learned a very great deal and have done so as active meaning-makers. In this they have been supported by parents who have, within their capabilities, been concerned to encourage their interests and initiatives and helped them to develop their skills and extend their thinking and language through conversation and joint activities. The fact that there are substantial differences between children in the extent to which their learning has progressed, just as there are differences between parents in their understanding of how best to give expression to their concern for their children's development, in no way invalidates the claims just made. The differences that undoubtedly exist are of degree rather than of kind.

Children's learning at home, however, because almost completely spontaneous, has been sporadic, unsystematic and, to a considerable extent, idiosyncratic. Starting school, with its opportunities for more systematic learning, would help them, we might hope:

- to go beyond the immediate event and the response it arouses, to set it in a wider context;
- to construct a broader and more coherent inner model, integrating new with old experience;
- to communicate through speech, and later through writing, with those who have had different experiences;

- to begin to reflect upon events, thoughts and feelings, and to use language to construct and explore imaginary and hypothetical 'possible worlds' – to engage in 'disembedded thinking'.

Such aims, it would seem, might ideally be best achieved by building upon what children already know and are able to do. Almost all children at this age have interests that can form the basis for activities which involve them in consolidating and developing existing knowledge and skills. Such interests can often also be seen to call for the acquisition of new skills and the obtaining of new knowledge. Equally, interests suggested by the teacher may be taken up by children and similarly form the basis for purposeful learning. Within such a framework there will be little need for the practising of isolated skills, for children will be keen to learn basic skills in order successfully to attain goals that they have had some responsibility for setting themselves. Learning to read is not a chore if the content of what is read is necessary for a project to which the child is committed. Similarly, adding and subtracting are skills worth acquiring if they are necessary for running a shop, making a working model or solving an intriguing problem arising from observations of the environment. And the more competent that children become, the more challenging are the tasks they are able to undertake and the broader the range of knowledge and skills they can develop as a result.

Furthermore, where the organization of the curriculum is seen in these terms and children are encouraged to take on a considerable measure of responsibility for choosing and carrying out the activities in which they engage in the classroom, the demand on the teacher to direct and monitor their every activity is removed. As a result, the teacher is freed for the more important tasks of sharing interests and enthusiasms and helping them to think and talk about what they are doing; helping them, that is:

- to articulate their aims and to formulate appropriate plans of action;
- to recognize problems and to consider alternative means of resolving them;
- to use available resources to the best effect, e.g. books, equipment and material;
- to evaluate the outcomes of their activities, both functionally and aesthetically.

As with parents who sustain and extend their children's interests in the pre-school years, this requires making time and space available for children to talk, and listening carefully to what they have to say, without immediately imposing an adult point of view. For such a response, with its implication that teacher really knows best, pre-empts the children's attempts and may thus undermine their confidence in their ability to work things out for themselves.

After the ability to listen attentively, the next most important skill that a teacher needs in order to talk productively with children is probably that of asking querstions – questions, that is, which foster the 'reflectiveness', that Bruner (1972) and others have seen as so important for intellectual growth. Such questions have as their aim to help the child to develop and explore his or her thinking through discussing it with a sympathetic and constructive listener. For such conversation to be successful, therefore, it is essential that teachers be genuinely interested in what children have to tell them and that they think of their questions, first and foremost, as a means of facilitating the children's communication.

There are undoubtedly many teachers who interact with children in this way, collaborating with them in their meaning-making whilst at the same time, by virtue of their professional expertise, helping them to extend their understanding further. However, it seems from our observations that this is the exception rather than the rule. Most teachers, it appears, are so anxious to turn every encounter with a child into an occasion for teaching or checking on prior learning that they only listen to the child's contribution long enough to decide how best to use it to advantage from their own adult point of view. The following is a typical example of such classroom conversation, even though it is child-initiated.

L: I want to show you! Isn't it big!   [Lee brings a chestnut]

T: It is big isn't it? What is it?

L: A conker

T: Yes

L: Then that'll need opening up

T: It needs opening up What does it need opening up for?

L: 'Cos the seed's inside

L: A conker

L: Horse chestnut

T: Yes very good
What will the seed grow into?

T: No it won't grow into a conker
It'll grow into a sort of tree won't it?
Can you remember the –

T: Horse chestnut Good
Put your conker on the nature table then

Our objection to this, and to countless other similar conversations that start from something in which the child is interested, is not that teachers are concerned to extend their pupils' knowledge (in informal as well as in formal situations), but that they are so concerned to do so that they never really discover what it is about the experience that the child finds sufficiently significant to want to share in the first place.

Children's experience of how adults engage in conversation with them in the years before they come to school has not been like this. The result is that many of them are bewildered by the new situation which they meet in the classroom, where they suddenly find themselves expected to fit in with someone else's definition of what is interesting and to learn what someone else prescribes. It is not surprising, therefore, that some children become tongue-tied and appear much less competent than they really are. (See the example of Rosie with Teacher A quoted in Chap.1.)

An indication of the sharpness of the transition is given by some statistics from a comparison we made between the language experience at home and school of the children in our full longitudinal study. Each child was recorded in his or her home a few weeks before starting school and then in the classroom half-way through the first term. An identical time-based sampling procedure was used in the two settings, so the data are strictly comparable. Only a quarter of the recordings have been analysed in full so far, however, so these results can only be treated as approximate. Nevertheless, the differences between home and school are striking.

As one might expect, even when all talk between adult and child is included – in group or whole class contexts as well as in one-to-one conversation – the amount of such talk is much less at school than at home (175 utterances addressed to an adult by the child at home, on average, compared with 30 utterances at school).

This is almost inevitable given the relative number of adults and children in the two settings. However the difference in ratio of adults to children does not, in itself, explain the other discrepancies: the small proportion of sequences initiated by the child at school, the infrequency of questions asked by the child and the high proportion of adult questions to the child which are 'display' questions, that is to say questions which call upon the respondent to display skill or knowledge rather than to supply information unknown to the questioner (see Table 1). But perhaps the most striking difference between the two settings is in the relative proportions of adult utterances which extend the child's topic and those which pursue a topic previously contributed by the adult. Children's experience at school in this respect is almost the exact reverse of their experience at home. Compared with parents, teachers, it appears, are typically far more concerned to pursue their own topics – to follow their own agenda – than to accept and extend the topics offered by the child.

Table 1 Comparison of children's language experience at home and at school: mean values

	Home	School
% of all adult–child sequences that are one-to-one	99	58*
% of sequences that are child-initiated	73	16*
% of child utterances to adult that are questions	12	3*
% of adult utterances that are questions	15	21
% of adult questions that are 'display' questions	20	52*
% of adult utterances that extend child's topic	38	14*
% of adult utterances that pursue adult topic	14	40*

*Differences significant at 1% level (Mann-Whitney U Test)

One reason for this overall low proportion of 'extending' utterances from teachers is that a large part of the child's interaction with the teacher – particularly sustained interaction – takes place in the context of group or whole class discussion. Such discussions form an integral part of almost every infant class's day, serving to achieve a corporate identity and providing an opportunity to create a shared experience. Furthermore, many teachers see such discussions as a means of developing children's ability to think and express themselves through language. However, in the light of the above statistics, we may question whether this latter aim is really achieved.

Consider the following example. Stella and her class-mates (aged 5–7 years) had, a few days previously, been on a visit to Berkeley Castle, where they had seen, among other things, the dungeon where Edward II was kept prisoner and finally murdered. They had also seen various historic artefacts and pieces of furniture. In the following excerpt from the discussion that followed their visit, the teacher chose to focus the children's attention on the four-poster bed.

T: Can anyone tell me WHY the bed's called a four-poster? [T holds up a picture of a four-poster bed]

C_1: Because it's <u>cold</u>

T: Put <u>up</u> – wait a minute
Put your hand up and I'll ask you
Stephen? (calling on S to answer)

S: Because it's got four posts

T: Four po- WHY has it got four posts?
Can anyone –
Put your hand up if you want to say [Several hands go up]
WHY has it got four posts?
I want all the little ones to try and think
Why has it got four posts?

–..–..–..–

162 *Language, Learning and Education*

[When the 'little ones' have failed to answer, Angela is called upon]

A: 'Cos it's got curtains

T: Yes it's got to hold the curtains hasn't it? What else has it got that needs four posts? [Several older children put hands up] Marion?

M: To hold it

T: Yes it's got a sort of roof – flat roof to it, hasn't it? Now let's think why the bed might have a roof on it Do you have a roof on your bed?

Ch: No (scornfully)

T: I wonder why

C: I dunno

T: I wonder why some of these four-poster beds had roofs on top of them I wonder why they would need a roof

C$_2$: I got a bunk bed

T: You've got a bunk – Well you HAVE got a roof on yours then haven't you? Are you on the top – <u>bunk</u> or the lower bunk?

C$_2$: <u>No</u> I'm on the bottom

T: Well then you've got a roof haven't you?

Cs: ⎧ I'm on the top
    ⎩ I'm on the bottom

T: Brian, why do you think they might need a roof on top of their bed?

B: Because there wasn't any fires in those days

T: In – where wasn't there any fires?

B: In the country

T: Yes but –

B: There wasn't any matches or any – um – wood

T: Well they <u>might have had wood to make a fire</u> mightn't they?

C: xxxx
   They had no matches

T: As a matter of fact I think they did – have – fires in this castle – some beautiful fireplaces

[T holds up a picture of one of the castle rooms]

T: There's one there

A: And one in the cooking room

T: Was there one in the bedroom?

A: No I don't expect there was

T: Well there may have been
There were sometimes
You can't see there but they did have fireplaces

> And they did have
> large pieces of wood
> on the fire to keep
> them warm
> So why do you think
> they needed a roof on
> their bed?

Finally, after a further 24 turns, the sought-for answer is given – by the teacher:

> They were very large rooms and the little tiny fireplaces probably didn't give enough heat
>
> So people had a roof on their bed and they drew the curtains round them and it was like being in a little – like a little tent

I quote this example at length because, in its tightness of focus and in its exploration of the implications of certain pupil contributions, it was one of the most successful discussions that we observed. But it also demonstrates some of the less desirable features which are so frequent in such discussions: teacher dominating, asking all the questions; pupils addressing their contributions – usually short, elliptical responses – to the teacher; only a minority actively participating; and the 'correct' answer, already preformulated in the mind of the teacher, acting like a beacon to which she steers the discussion, with little consideration being given to pupil contributions that, siren-like in their teacher-perceived irrelevance, might lure her off her chosen course.

It may be argued that such characteristics are almost inevitable when one adult is trying to coordinate the participation of 30 or so individuals who, by virtue of their immaturity, are still rarely capable of shaping their contributions to a mutually agreed topic. It would seem, therefore, that if teachers really wish to develop children's linguistic abilities – to help them to express their ideas coherently and fluently, and to listen carefully and critically to the contributions of others – they should do so in one-to-one, or at most small group, situations, where a greater reciprocity of interaction is possible, and where the children can try out their ideas in a tentative manner, free from the pressures felt by both child and teacher in the large group situation.

If, on the other hand, the teacher's primary aim is to impart information, this would surely be more effectively achieved by her telling the children what it is she wants them to know. This would leave more time for them to respond with comments and questions if they wished to do so – though even this would probably be more successful with a small group rather than with the whole class.

For a skilled teacher, particularly when interacting with individual pupils, it is certainly possible to have sustained and constructive discussion, to which the pupil as well as the teacher contributes matter of substance and relevance. In the following example, taken from a conversation between Kim (aged seven) and her teacher, the topic is the illustrated nature diary that Kim is making, inspired by Edith Holden's *Diary of a Country Lady*.*

In this extract we can see how the teacher's questions, asked with a genuine interest in how the child had set about her work, prompt Kim to think more deeply about what she has been doing in order to explain it to somebody else. On another occasion the teacher might well have chosen to extend the intellectual or technical aspects of Kim's work, by talking, for example, about the refraction of light that caused the 'bend' that Kim had captured in her painting, or the techniques available for representing depth, needed to convey the three-dimensional relationships among the leaves. My reason for choosing this extract, however, is that it illustrates how the kind of teacher–pupil talk I have been discussing can contribute to children's affective and aesthetic development as well as to that of the intellect.

T: That's a lovely page isn't it? Lovely Were you pleased with it?

K: Yes

T: What were you trying to do . . when you painted your forsythia? Do you remember what you were thinking about?

K: Like the real actual feeling?

T: How did that make you feel?

---

*This and the following example from a London school were brought to my attention by Moira McKenzie, who used them in her ETV series *Extending Literacy*. I am grateful for her permission to include the material here.

K: Make it. . .as it
stands. . .
perfectly the
same standing
position

T: I was interested that it [T tracing her
bent like that finger along
stem]
Did you see it bend
like that?
Did you look at that
part particularly?
[They turn over
And what about this? to page with
yellow
polyanthus]

K: Well
Me and Yelshea
wanted to do this
'cos it gave it a
lovely smell and
. . . it was um –
kind of beautiful. .
a lovely feeling
about it

T: Smashing
And on this page [T turns page]
Would you like to tell
me what you're doing
now?

K: Orange plant

T: Can I see your painting
of it – your drawing? [K shows orange
plant painting.
It has not yet
been stuck into
the diary]
Did you try with that
to get exactly the same
position? (i.e. as the
pot is in now)
Would you like to tell
me about your
drawing?

K: Well
Just um – the bottom bit was about the easiest thing I could do
So I done that pot first and I done it half way round
And then when I drew the pot I put the background of the pink bit and like down there
You think that was – um – covered like that but it isn't it's inside. .
And I done the pot . . . I couldn't find brown so I got grey
And . . I done the leaf like they should be and that one was about the hardest 'cos it had to blend . . . them two
And that's the background of the plant
There's a blue paper . . .
And that's all about the thing I done

[K points to leaf on plant]

T: Lovely
You managed very well to get that leaf

168 *Language, Learning and Education*

                              looking like it was curling over didn't you?
                              And how are you going to arrange this page? What's going to go on it?

K: Well
     If I – I'll have to cut it because there won't be enough room for the book

                              [The paper with picture of orange plant]

     So I'll have to. . get it . . . a sort of pattern like that to make sure the thing go in

                              [K indicates the shape of paper on previous page]

The conversation from which this extract is taken lasted more than five minutes. Yet while the teacher was talking to Kim there were almost no interruptions. The other children in the class were busily occupied on their own tasks, working individually or in groups of twos and threes. Such a pattern of working clearly requires considerable preparation and organization. But, even more importantly, it involves a particular attitude to the teacher–pupil relationship. It is to this that we shall now turn.

Talking, Thinking and the Curriculum

As we have just seen, compared with whole-class discussion, one-to-one interaction provides a much better opportunity for the negotiation of meaning and purpose on which the development of language so largely depends. But whole-class discussion has other disadvantages. Because large group sessions are often the means whereby children are introduced to new ideas and invited to respond to new experiences, the prevalence of a teacher-dominated style of interaction frequently means that it is only the teacher's curriculum-based perspective on the topic that is treated as relevant. What is expected of the children is that they should follow the teacher's line of thinking and their contributions tend to be evaluated solely in this light.

Where this is the case, quite unintended messages may be conveyed to children about the nature of learning, as engaged in at school, namely that:

- the only valid learning is that which takes place when children are engaged in teacher-prescribed tasks;
- personal experience, particularly that gained outside the classroom, is unlikely in the teacher's eyes to be of relevance for learning;
- taking the initiative is discouraged; as thinking things out for oneself may lead to incorrect answers, it is better to play safe and try only to follow the steps laid down by the teacher;
- children are not capable of taking responsibility for self-directed learning: they are only expected to work productively and effectively when they are closely directed and supervised.

Few teachers really wish children to see school in this light; yet many interact with their pupils in ways that make it likely that the pupils will come to be passive, if not recalcitrant, learners. However, if we look back to the years before school, it is clear that this need not be the case. In the first few years of life a quite remarkable amount of active learning takes place, as children learn their native language and simultaneously learn about the world through interacting with other people through language. From our observations, it is quite evident that there is no need at this stage for strongly directed teaching or for constant evaluation. Children are innately predisposed to make sense of their experience, to pose problems for themselves and actively to search for and achieve solutions. They also show considerable perseverence in such activities when the challenge is of their own choosing.

These qualities are very much in evidence in the pre-school years. Surely, therefore, they should form the foundation upon which the curriculum is constructed at school. If we believe that language and learning continue to be intimately related throughout the years of schooling – and it would be difficult to argue otherwise – a major principle in planning and implementing the curriculum must be to ensure that pupils are encouraged to pursue and extend their own interests and given the opportunity, wherever possible, to share responsibility for the formulation, execution and evaluation of the learning tasks in which they engage.

Most nursery, infant and junior teachers already subscribe to these aims but, in practice, they often get displaced by the concern to ensure that the curriculum is covered in a systematic manner. In recent years, much effort has been devoted to the analysis of learning tasks into small, relatively self-contained steps so that they can be arranged in a linear sequence for the purposes of teaching. This has led to an exaggerated belief in the value of structured and graded curricula. The problem with this approach is that, whilst certain types of learning *can* effectively be promoted in this way, it is certainly not the case that children only learn – or even learn best – when *all* the tasks in which they engage are imposed on them by others in the interests of ensuring uniform progression through a predetermined sequence. And as regards learning the language with which to learn, it is clearly not the case at all.

All of us – adults and children alike – learn most effectively when we are working on a task or problem to which we have a personal commitment, either because the goal is one that we are determined to achieve (the completion of a painting, poem or model) or because the problem is one that we find intrinsically fascinating. When engaged in such tasks, as the example with Kim shows, discussion with someone more skilled takes on real meaning and purpose, as progress to date is reviewed and alternative plans for further work are considered in terms of their feasibility and appropriateness. In such contexts, talking and learning are integrated in the pursuit of the goal to which they are both instrumental.

This can be seen happening very clearly in the following example, as Colin (another seven-year-old in the same class as Kim) discusses with his teacher how he is going to set about making the tripod for his model camera. Once again, the focus is on helping the child to think through and explain his plan, but notice how the teacher takes the opportunity to suggest the use of reference books – which she had made sure will be to hand when they are needed. By drawing attention to the usefulness of reading, calculating dimensions and recording work done in various ways, she is ensuring that 'basic skills' are not neglected, but is emphasizing their importance in a context in which the child can immediately see their relevance.

T: Colin, are you having a problem?
C: Just trying to – think out – something

	Just trying to think out how high I want the pole			
		T:	Could you work there a while. I'll just help Colin	[to another child]
C:	One metre and –			[T joins Colin who is using a metre stick, extending it with a small ruler]
		T:	Can you imagine for a minute that you're taking a photograph?	
			How high would be comfortable?	
C:	Er – this is what I done – trying to find out I put this like that and held it and just pretend I was looking through And I thought I'd have it about that high 'cos that could include the camera on top and that's how far I want it – one metre and thirteen –			[C indicates that this is what he is already trying to do] [C counts on small ruler]
	One metre and thirteen centimetres			
		T:	Is that going to be the height of your tripod?	
C:	Yes – of the pole			
		T:	Is each pole going to be that height?	
C:	I'm only going to have three um – yes			

C: The other two are going to be a bit longer

T: Can you show me how you're going to do your plan?

C: I've got –

T: Sit yourself down

C: I've got a (lump) of wood

T: Pardon?

C: I've got some wood – and that's what it's going to look like [C shows his plan]

It's going to have those bits so I can put something round it to hold the camera on and – I'm going to try and get something that can – a round hole – but that could hold on – on legs – which is going to be rather hard

T: Have you looked in the camera book to see if it shows a diagram that would help you?

C: Er – I have looked in one

T: Did you notice that there was another one there today?

C: No
Yes there is [C looks]

T: Perhaps in a moment you'd like to look at that – that might be helpful

C: Yes

Such talk is most aptly described as negotiating. And in this particular class it occurs not only whilst pupils are engaged in particular tasks but also at the stage when the work for the week is being planned. Of course there are some types of learning that the teacher has to ensure are undertaken regularly and systematically – mastering arithmetic skills, principles of spelling, and so on – but these, although essential, occupy only a relatively small part of each day. For the rest of the time, children engage in a wide variety of tasks that they have chosen to undertake in discussion with the teacher. Some of them arise from interests that originate with the children – Colin's camera and tripod, for example; others arise from topics and materials introduced by the teacher – for example, the nature study and recording associated with the *Diary of a Country Lady*.

Whatever the origin, though, what is important is that the children are engaged in tasks that they have taken on and *made their own*. The result is a commitment to the task that enables them to work without close supervision; and this in turn frees the teacher to spend considerable periods of time with individual children when they really need help or want to talk about what they are doing.

Putting Intentions into Practice

Teaching in this way – negotiating the curriculum – is not easy, of course. For it requires a considerable degree of flexibility and preparedness to meet the very varied interests that one's pupils propose to pursue. It also demands a constant state of open receptiveness to pupils' ideas – a willingness to see things from another point of view which, although less mature and often by adult standards misguided or simply wrong, has its own validity as the most meaningful interpretation that can be achieved by a particular pupil at this stage in his or her development. It also requires imagination to find new activities, themes and materials which will spark off fresh interests and make connections between those that are already being developed.

Some teachers may perhaps feel that they are simply unable to meet such demands: that the breadth of their general knowledge is insufficient, or that they lack some of the necessary skills. Some may feel that, with so many pupils each engaged in different activities, things may get out of control. Such doubts are understandable and certainly very real. But, as the previous examples show, they are likely to be based on an underestimate of children's willingness and ability to work responsibly and productively without close supervision, and on a misconception of the teacher's role in the teacher–pupil relationship.

It is not necessary for a teacher personally to know all the answers to pupils' questions or to be already competent in all the skills that an open curriculum may call for. Indeed, a teacher who is universally knowledgeable and competent may offer a model which actually makes it more difficult for pupils to gain confidence in their ability to learn *on their own*. Learning is first and foremost a process – a continuous making of meanings and an adding to and restructuring of the internal model of the world that each individual has already built up. The product is, in many cases, of less importance. For, if the process has been mastered, it is always possible to remake the product, if and when the occasion demands.

Furthermore, since this process is essentially interactive, it is more helpful for the apprentice learner to work with teachers who are themselves still actively engaged in learning – to collaborate with them in formulating real problems and posing real questions and then in considering with them how to set about finding solutions and answers – than it is to be directed and evaluated by those who apparently no longer themselves have the need to engage in such processes.

What I am calling for, therefore, is a fundamental re-examination of what it means to be a teacher. Part of the answer, of course, has to do with being well informed about the content of the curriculum and its organization. Much attention is currently being given to such matters and teachers are rightly being encouraged to rethink their teaching from this point of view. But just as important is the *style of interaction* that the teacher adopts in mediating between the content of the curriculum and the pupils for whose learning he or she is responsible. This aspect of teaching, however, has received much less attention. Yet when teachers have an opportunity to examine their behaviour objectively they are often surprised and shocked to discover 'the enormous gap between intention and realization', as one teacher put it. This is very understandable. The pressures on teachers to retreat to a 'transmission' style of teaching are great and continually increasing. But in the long run, I would contend, such a style is ultimately self-defeating, because it fails to recognize the true nature of the learning process.

Teaching, I have argued, should start with a recognition that children are already active, self-directed learners outside the classroom and should seek to foster these same qualities inside the classroom, whilst at the same time helping them to develop a broader range of interests and more powerful skills and strategies for exploring them. This, I have suggested, can best be achieved when learning is seen as a joint activity in which teachers and pupils collaborate; and since this collaboration finds its expression most naturally through conversation, it is to ways of talking and listening that I have sought chiefly to draw attention.

One important question remains: what are the practical steps that need to be taken to turn ideals into reality? That this is a very real problem for many teachers has already been recognized. But, even if space permitted, no simple answer could be given. For, in the end, the only really satisfactory solution is the one that each teacher works out for him or herself, taking into account the children concerned, their parents, the school and its resources and environment. However, teachers have a great deal to learn from each other, and the most satisfying outcome of this chapter for the writer would be to see groups of teachers meeting together in their schools and local teachers' centres to share their ideas and experiences with each other. In the final analysis, it is the attitude that we ourselves adopt to learning that is the key. When we recognize that the learner must take responsibility for his or her own learning, we shall not only find that the answers to the practical questions are more likely to come from collaborative interaction with our colleagues than from some 'expert', but we shall also be practising ourselves the principles that we wish to implement in our classrooms.

Acknowledgement

I have benefited greatly in the writing of this chapter from discussions with colleagues, teachers and students taking the MEd. course in Language and Learning at the University of Bristol. In particular, I have received helpful comments and suggestions from: Dave Ellerby, John Nicholls, Elizabeth Robinson, Maggie Turner, Jan Wells and Rosemary Whitehurst. Although I have not always agreed with their suggestions, the arguments presented here would have been very different without them. I am very grateful for this opportunity to engage in collaborative learning.

Appendix 1

Bristol Language Development Programme

Conventions and Layout for Transcription

The speech of the child being studied is set out in the left hand column. The speech of all other participants is set out in the centre column, with identifying initials where necessary. Each new utterance starts on a new line.

Contextual information is enclosed in square brackets [] and set out in the right hand column.

Interpretations of utterances and descriptions of tone of voice, where applicable, are enclosed in round brackets () and included immediately after the utterance to which they apply.

Utterances, or parts of utterances, about which there is doubt are enclosed in angular brackets ‹›; where two interpretations are possible they are both given, separated by an oblique stroke.

Symbols of the International Phonetic Alphabet are used for utterances, or parts of utterances, which cannot be interpreted with certainty. Phonetic symbols are always enclosed by oblique strokes. Except where there is doubt about the speaker's intended meaning, the speech is transcribed in Standard English Orthography.

The following is a list of additional symbols used, with an explanation of their significance. (Stops and commas are not used as in normal punctuation.)

?   used at end of any utterance where an interrogative meaning is considered to have been intended.

!   used at the end of an utterance considered to have exclamatory intention.

'   apostrophe: used as normal for contractions and elision of syllables.

*	used to indicate unintelligibility, for whatever reason. The number of asterisks corresponds as nearly as possible to the number of words judged to have been uttered.
. . .	stops are used to indicate pauses. One stop is used for a very short pause. Thereafter, the number of stops used corresponds to the estimated length of the pause in seconds. Pauses over five seconds in length are shown with the figure for the length of the pause, e.g. . . .8. .
—	underlining. Where utterances overlap because both speakers speak at once, the overlapping portions are underlined.
" "	inverted commas are used to enclose utterances considered to be 'speech for self'
+	plus mark indicated unbroken intonation contour where a pause or clause boundary might otherwise indicate the end of an utterance.
–	hyphen indicates a hiatus, either because the utterance is incomplete or because the speaker makes a fresh start at the word or utterance.
(v)	used to indicate that the preceding word was used as a vocative, to call or hold the attention of the addressee.

Intonation

Some of the transcripts include a representation of intonation, in which case the following additional conventions apply:

//	Tone unit boundary. Where an utterance consists of only one tone unit, no boundaries are marked.
'	This symbol immediately precedes both prominent and tonic syllables. Prominent syllables [1] take a single digit before the word in which they occur to indicate their relative pitch height.

CAPS	Tonic syllables [2] are printed in capitals; they also take two or more digits before the word to indicate the onset level, range and direction of significant pitch movement (see 'Pitch Height' below)
↑ ↓	Shift of pitch range relatively higher or lower than that normal for the speaker.
↑↑ ↓↓	Shift to extra high or low pitch.
:	Lengthened syllable. The symbol follows the syllable to which it applies.
Pitch Height	The height, direction and range of significant pitch movement is represented by a set of digits corresponding to points on a scale. The pitch range of a speaker is divided into five notional bands, numbered 1–5 from high to low, thus:

```
─────────────────────
       1
─────────────────────
          2
─────────────────────
             3
─────────────────────
                4
─────────────────────
                   5
─────────────────────
```

The following information is retrievable from this coding:

Direction of Movement	Halliday (1967) Tones
Falling: (e.g. 13, 25)	Tone 1
Rising: (e.g. 31, 43)	Tone 2
Level: (e.g. 33)	Tone 3
Fall-Rise: (e.g. 343 or (e.g. 342)	Tone 4 or Tone 2[3]
Rise-Fall: (e.g. 324)	Tone 5

Notes:
1. Prominent syllables are salient with respect to combinations of pitch, duration and intensity.

2. Tonic syllables carry at least the onset of significant pitch movement. Significant pitch movement in its entirety may, of course, occur on a single syllable or be spread over a number of syllables.

3. Fall-Rise movements may be of two types, corresponding to Halliday's Tone 2 and Tone 4. They are conventionally denoted in the transcripts as follows: Tone 2 is represented with a higher terminal pitch than its onset (e.g. 342), whereas Tone 4 is represented as having a terminal pitch no higher than its onset (e.g. 232, 354).

Reference: HALLIDAY, M.A.K. (1967). *Intonation and Grammar in British English,* Atlantic Highlands, N.J.: Humanities Press.

Appendix 2

Name: Sally Date of Birth: 8.4.70
Date of Recording: 10.1.75 Record. No. 7

Sample No. 8 Participants: Mother, Sally Location: Kitchen
Time: 11.57
Activity: Mother is cooking.
Sally is watching.

S: Ma (v) [Radio on]
I've got a * cos. I
didn't – I – that
make me sick
that do

        (no response)

S: Ma (v) can I go
out?

M: No
It's cold out now
One two three four [M counts
five six seven eight before lighting
nine ten (sings) the gas stove]

S: Mum (v) what we
got?

        (no response)

S: Mum (v) let me
have a look
what's burning
Mm (v) that egg's
burning in'it?

M: What?

S: That egg's
burning

        . .

S: Oh Mum (v) !
(with consternation)
Which – where
my egg?

        (no response)

S: Mum (v) we both
got to have eggs

M: I'll be a bag of nerves
if you don't shut up
(shouts)
. . .

S: Mum (v)
Lift your bag up
(no response)
S: Oh! what's that?
"*****‹all the food›"
**
Mum (v) we
both – [M beating eggs]

Sample No. 9 Participants: Sally, Mother Location: Kitchen
Time: 12.07
Activity: Mother is preparing.
Sally is watching

S: "Oh"
. .
. .4. .
M: What you doing?
(no response)
M: You do it the hard
way don't you?
(no response)
. .
S: "Don't fall out" [S doesn't seem
Ah! baked to expect any
potato! answers]
****
. .6. .
M: Oh God!
. .7. .
S: That egg and
chips

. .
S: That egg is dirty
Mummy (v)
(no response)
. .6. .
S: Oh! bacon!
Now what's this? [S mistakes
chops for bacon]

                              M: What! (exclamation)
                                 You got bacon on the
                                 mind or summat?
           (no response)
                                 ..5..
S: "Oh"
                              M: Right take a stool in
                                 now ** ready yet
                                 ..
S: Mum (v) this is a
   pancake
   Pancakes
                              M: It's not a pancake
                                 It's an omelette
                                 (brusquely)
S: Omelette (repeats)
   O-o-o-o
   Omelette omelette
   I likes omelette

References

AINSWORTH, M.D.S., BELL, S.M. and STAYTON, D.J. (1974). 'Infant-mother attachment and social development: socialisation as a product of reciprocal responsiveness to signals'. In: RICHARDS, M.P.M. (Ed) *The Integration of a Child into a Social World.* Cambridge: Cambridge University Press.

BARNES, D. (1971). *Language, the Learner and the School.* (revd. edition) Harmondsworth: Penguin.

BARNES, D. (1976). *From Communication to Curriculum.* Harmondsworth: Penguin.

BARNES, S.B., GUTFREUND, M., SATTERLY, D.J. and WELLS, C.G. (1983). 'Characteristics of adult speech which predict children's language development', *Journal of Child Language*, 10, 65–84.

BATES, E. AND MACWHINNEY, B. (1982). 'Functionalist approaches to grammar'. In: WANNER, E. and GLEITMAN, L.R. (Eds) *Language Acquisition: the State of the Art.* Cambridge: Cambridge University Press.

BEREITER, C. et al. (1966). 'An academically oriented pre-school for culturally deprived children'. In: HECHINGER, F.M. (Ed) *Pre-School Education Today.* New York: Doubleday.

BERNSTEIN, B. (1971). *Class, Codes and Control,* Vol. 1. London: Routledge and Kegan Paul.

BERNSTEIN, B. (Ed) (1973). *Class, Codes and Control,* Vol. II, *Applied Studies Towards a Sociology of Language.* London: Routledge and Kegan Paul.

BERNSTEIN, B. (1977). Foreword, in: ADLAM, D.C., *Code in Context.* London: Routledge and Kegan Paul.

BOWERMAN, M. (1982). 'Reorganizational processes in language development'. In: WANNER, E. and GLEITMAN, L.R. (Eds) *Language Acquisition: the State of the Art.* Cambridge: Cambridge University Press.

BRIMER, M.A. and DUNN, L. (1963). *English Picture Vocabulary Test.* Windsor: NFER–NELSON

BROWN, R. (1958). *Words and Things.* Glencoe: Free Press.

BROWN, R. (1973) *A First Language: the Early Stages.* London: George Allen and Unwin.

BROWN, R. (1977). Introduction. In: SNOW, C.E. and FERGUSON, C.A. (Eds) *Talking with Children: From Input to Acquisition*. Cambridge: Cambridge University Press.

BROWN, R. and BELLUGI, U. (1964). 'Three Processes in the Child's Acquisition of Syntax', *Harvard Educational Review*, 34, 133–151.

BROWN, R., CAZDEN, C. and BELLUGI, U. (1969). 'The Child's Grammar from I to III'. In: HILL, J.P. (Ed) *The Second Annual Minnesota Symposium on Child Psychol.* Minneapolis: University of Minnesota Press.

BRUNER, J.S. (1972). *The Relevance of Education*. Harmondsworth: Penguin.

BRUNER, J.S. (1975). 'The ontogenesis of speech acts', *Journal of Child Language*, 2, 1, 1–20.

BRUNER, J.S. (1981). The pragmatics of acquisition. In: DEUTSCH, W. (Ed) *The Child's Construction of Language*. London: Academic Press.

CAREY, S. (1978). 'The child as word learner'. In: HALLE, M., BRESNAN, J. and MILLER, G.A. (Eds) *Linguistic Theory and Psychological Reality*. Cambridge, Mass.: M.I.T. Press.

CAZDEN, C.B. (1973). Play with Language and Metalinguistic Awareness: one dimension of language experience. Paper presented at the second Lucy Sprague Mitchell Memorial Conference: 'Dimensions of Language Experience', Bank Street College of Education, 19 May 1973.

CAZDEN, C.B. (1976). 'How knowledge about language, helps the classroom teacher – or does it? a personal account', *The Urban Review*, Summer 1976.

CHAFE, W. (1970). *Meaning and the Structure of Language*. Chicago: University of Chicago Press.

CHOMSKY, N.A. (1959). Review of SKINNER, B.F. Verbal Behaviour *Language*, 35, 26–58.

CHOMSKY, N.A. (1964). Discussion of Miller and Ervin's Paper. In: BELLUGI, U. and BROWN, R. (Eds) *The Acquisition of Language*. Monogr. Soc. Res. Child Development, 29, No. 1, 35–42.

CHOMSKY, N.A. (1965). *Aspects of the Theory of Syntax*. Cambridge, Mass.: M.I.T. Press.

CHOMSKY, N.A. (1966). Linguistic theory. Paper presented at the North-East Conference on Research and Language Learning.

CHOMSKY, N.A. (1976). *Reflections on Language*. London: Fontana.

CLARK, R. (1974). 'Performing without competence', *Journal of Child Language* 1, 1, 1–10.

CLARK, R. (1975). Some even simpler ways to learn to talk. Paper presented at the Third International Child Language Symposium. London, September 1975.

CLAY, M.M. (1972a). *Reading: the Patterning of Complex Behaviour*. London: Heinemann

CLAY, M.M. (1972b). *The Early Detection of Reading Difficulties: a diagnostic survey*. London: Heinemann Educational.

COOK-GUMPERZ, J., GUMPERZ, J.J. and SIMON, H.D. (1979). *Language at School and Home: Theory, Methods and Preliminary Findings.* Unpublished report, University of California, Berkeley.

CROSS, T.G. (1977). 'Mothers' speech adjustments: the contribution of selected child listener variables'. In: SNOW, C.E. and FERGUSON, C.A. (Eds) *Talking to Children: Language Input and Acquisition* Cambridge: Cambridge University Press.

CROSS, T.G. (1978). 'Mother's speech and its association with rate of linguistic development in young children'. In WATERSON, N. and SNOW, C.E. (Eds) *The Development of Communication.* Chichester: Wiley.

CRYSTAL, D. (1975). *The English Tone of Voice.* London: Edward Arnold.

CRYSTAL, D., FLETCHER, P. and GARMAN, M. (1976). *The Grammatical Analysis of Language Disability: A Procedure for Assessment and Remediation. 'Studies in Language Disability and Remediation'.* London: Edward Arnold.

DAVIES, B. (1980). 'An analysis of primary children's account of classroom interaction', *British Journal of Sociology of Education,* I, 257–278.

DEUTSCH, W. (1981). Introduction. In: DEUTSCH, W. (Ed) *The Child's Construction of Language.* London: Academic Press.

DONALDSON, M. (1966). Discussion of MCNEILL (1966) 'The Creation of Language'. In: LYONS, J. and WALES, R.J. (Eds) *Psycholinguistics Papers.* Edinburgh: Edinburgh University Press.

DONALDSON, M. (1978). *Children's Minds.* London: Fontana.

DORE, J. (1975). 'Holophrases, speech acts and language universals', *Journal of Child Language,* 2: 21–40.

EDWARDS, A.D. (1976). *Language in Culture and Class.* London: Heinemann Educational.

EDWARDS, D. (1973). 'Sensory–motor intelligence and semantic relations in early child grammar', *Cognition,* 2, 395–434.

ERVIN-TRIPP, S.M. (1978). 'Some features of early child–adult dialogue', *Language in Society,* 7, 357–73.

ERVIN-TRIPP, S.M. (1980). 'Speech acts, social meaning and social learning'. In: GILES, H., ROBINSON, W.P. and SMITH, P.M. (Eds) *Language: Social Psychological Perspectives.* Oxford: Pergamon.

EVANS, R. et al. (1978). *Swansea Evaluation Profile for School Entrants* (for researchers). Windsor: NFER–NELSON

FERRIER, LINDA (1978). 'Some observations of error in context'. In: WATERSON, N. and SNOW, C.E. (Eds) *The Development of Communication.* New York: Wiley.

FILLMORE, C.J. (1968). 'The case for case'. In: BACH, E. and HARMS, R.T. (Eds) *Universals in Linguistic Theory.* New York: Holt Rinehart.

FRENCH, P. and MACLURE, M. (1980). 'Getting the right answer and getting the answer right', *Research in Education,* 22, 1–23.

FROSTIG, M. and HORNE, D. (1973). *Frostig Program for the Development of Visual Perception: teachers' guide.* Chicago: Follett.

FURROW, D., NELSON, K. and BENEDICT, H. (1979). 'Mothers' speech to children and syntactic development: some simple relationships', *Journal of Child Language*, 6, 423–442.

GOODMAN, Y.M. and BURKE, C.L. (1972). *Reading Miscue Inventory: Procedure for Diagnosis and Evaluation*. New York: Macmillan.

GRIFFITHS, P. (1979). Speech acts and early sentences. In: FLETCHER, P. and GARMAN, M. (Eds) *Language Acquisition*. Cambridge: Cambridge University Press.

HALLIDAY, M.A.K. (1968). 'Language and experience', *Educational Review*, 20, 2, 95–106.

HALLIDAY, M.A.K. (1975). *Learning How to Mean*. London: Edward Arnold.

HALLIDAY, M.A.K. (1978). *Language as Social Semiotic*. London: Edward Arnold.

HEATH, S.B. (1983). *Ways with Words*. Cambridge: Cambridge University Press.

HOCKING, M. (1977). Verbal Interaction in the Infant Classroom and Its Place in the Learning Process. Unpublished Ph.D. thesis, University of Bristol.

INGRAM, E. (1969). Language Development in Children. In: FRASER, H. and O'DONNELL, W.R. (Eds) *Applied Linguistics and the Teaching of English*. London: Longman.

KAYE, K. and CHARNEY, R. (1980). 'How mothers maintain dialogue with two-year olds'. In: OLSON, D. (Ed) *The Social Foundations of Language and Thought*. New York: Norton.

LABOV, W. (1970). 'The logic of non-standard English'. In: WILLIAMS, F. (Ed) *Language and Poverty*. Chicago: Markham Publishing Co.

LEE, LAURA L. (1970). 'A Screening Test for Syntax Development', *Journal of Speech and Hearing Disorders*, 35 (2), 103–112.

LIEVEN, E. (1978). 'Conversations between mothers and young children: individual differences and their possible implications for the study of language learning'. In: WATERSON, N. and SNOW, C.E. (Eds) *The Development of Communication*. New York: Wiley.

LOBAN, W.D. (1963). *The Language of Elementary School Children*. Champaign, Illinois: NCTE.

LOCK, A. (Ed) (1978). *Action, Gesture and Symbol – The Emergence of Language*. London: Academic Press.

LOCK, A. (1980). *The Guided Reinvention of Language*. London: Academic Press.

LORD, J.V. and BURROWAY, J. (1980). *The Giant Jam Sandwich*. London: Picture Piccolo Books.

MACLURE, M. and FRENCH, P. (1981). 'Talk at home and at school'. In: WELLS, C.G. *Learning through Interaction: the Study of Language Development*. Cambridge: Cambridge University Press.

MCCARTHY, D. (1930). *The Language Development of the Pre-School Child*. (Inst. of Child Welfare Monogr. Ser. No. 4) Minneapolis: University of Minnesota Press.

MCCARTHY, D. (1954). Language Development In Children. In: CARMICHAEL, L. (Ed) *Manual of Child Psychology*. New York: Wiley.

MCSHANE, J. (1980). *Learning to Talk*. Cambridge: Cambridge University Press.

MEEK, M. (1985). 'Play and paradoxes: some considerations of imagination and language'. In: WELLS, C.G. and NICHOLLS, J.C. (Eds) *Language and Learning: an Interactional Perspective*. Lewes, Sussex: Falmer Press.

MEHAN, H. (1979). *Learning Lessons, Social Organization in the Classroom*. Cambridge Mass.: Harvard University Press.

MESSNER, D.J. (1968). 'The integration of mothers' joint speech with joint play', *Journal of Child Development*, 49, 781–7.

MOON, C. (1976). *Pre-School Reading Experience and Learning to Read*. Unpublished M.Ed. dissertation, University of Bristol, School of Education.

NEALE, M.D. (1969). *Neale Analysis of Reading Ability* (2nd Ed). Basingstoke: Macmillan Education.

NELSON, K. (1973). Structure and strategy in learning to talk. *Monographs of the Society for Research in Child Development*, 38, 1–2 Ser. No. 149.

NEWPORT, E.L., GLEITMAN, H. and GLEITMAN, L.R. (1977). 'Mother, I'd rather do it myself: some effects and non-effects of maternal speech style'. In: SNOW, C.E. and FERGUSON, C.A. (Eds) *Talking to Children: Language Input and Acquisition*. Cambridge: Cambridge University Press.

NEWSON, J. (1978). Dialogue and development. In: LOCK, A. (Ed) *Action, Gesture and Symbol*. London: Academic Press.

NINIO, A. and BRUNER, J.S. (1978). 'The achievement and antecedents of labelling', *Journal of Child Language*, 5, 1–16.

OLSON, D. (1977). 'From utterance to text: the bias of language in speech and writing', *Harvard Educational Review*, 47, 3, 257–281.

PIAGET, J. (1926). *The Language and Thought of the Child*. London: Kegan Paul.

RABAN, B. (1975). *Self and Self-Concept*. Unpublished M.Ed. Dissertation, University of Bristol, School of Education.

RATNER, N. and BRUNER, J.S. (1978). 'Games, social exchange and the acquisition of language'. *Journal of Child Language*, 5, 391–401.

ROBINSON, W.P. (1978). *Language Management in Education: The Australian Context*. Sydney: George Allen and Unwin.

ROSCH, E. (1977). 'Classification of real-world objects: origins and representation in cognition'. In: JOHNSON-LAIRD, P.N. and WATSON, P.C. (Eds) *Thinking*. Cambridge: Cambridge University Press.

SACHS, J. (1977). 'The adaptive significance of linguistic input to pre-linguistic infants'. In: SNOW, C.E. and FERGUSON, C.A. (Eds) *Talking to Children: From Input to Acquisition.* Cambridge: Cambridge University Press.

SCOLLON, R. and SCOLLON, S.B.K. (1981). *Narrative, Literacy and Face in Interethnic Communication.* Norwood, N.J.: Ablex.

SHATZ, M. (1978). 'The development of communicative understanding: an early strategy for interpreting and responding to messages', *Cognitive Psychology*, 10, 271–301.

SHATZ, M. (1982). 'On mechanisms of language acquisition: Can features of the communicative environment account for development?' In: WANNER, E. and GLEITMAN, L.R. (Eds) *Language Acquisition: the State of the Art.* Cambridge: Cambridge University Press.

SHULTZ, J.J., FLORIO, S. and ERICKSON, F. (1982) '"Where's the floor?": aspects of the cultural organization of social relationships in communication at home and at school'. In: GILMORE, P. and GLATTHORN, A. (Eds) *Children In and Out of School: Ethnography and Education.* Washington, D.C.: Center for Applied Linguistics.

SINCLAIR, J. MCH. and COULTHARD, R.M. (1975). *Towards an Analysis of Discourse: the English used by Teachers and Pupils.* London: Oxford University Press.

SKINNER, B.F. (1957). *Verbal Behavior.* New York: Appleton.

SLOBIN, D.I. (1981). 'The origin of grammatical encoding of events'. In: DEUTSCH, W. (Ed) *The Child's Construction of Language.* London: Academic Press.

SNOW, C.E. (1976). 'The language of the mother–child relationship.' In: ROGERS, S. (Ed) *They Don't Speak Our Language.* London: Edward Arnold.

SNOW, C.E. (1977). 'Mothers' speech research: from input to interaction'. In: SNOW, C.E. and FERGUSON, C.A. (Eds) *Talking to Children: From Input to Acquisition.* Cambridge: Cambridge University Press.

SNOW, C.E. and FERGUSON, C.A. (Eds) (1977). *Talking to Children: Language Input and Acquisition.* Cambridge: Cambridge University Press.

SPENCER, M. (1976). 'Stories are for telling', *English in Education*, 10, 16–23.

STERN, D. (1977). *The First Relationship: Infant and Mother.* London: Open Books.

TEMPLIN, M.C. (1957). *Certain Language Skills in Children.* Minneapolis: University of Minnesota.

TOUGH, J. (1973). 'The language of young children: the implications for the education of the young disadvantaged child'. In: CHAZAN, M. (Ed) *Education in the Early Years.* Swansea: University College of Swansea, Faculty of Education.

TOUGH, J. (1977). *The Development of Meaning.* London: Unwin Education Books.

References

TREVARTHEN, C. (1969). 'Communication and Cooperation in Early Infancy A Description of Primary Intersubjectivity'. In: BULLOWA, M. (Ed) *Before Speech: The Beginnings of Human Communication.* Cambridge: Cambridge University Press.

VYGOTSKY, L.S. (1977). *Thinking and Speech.* Selected passages of *Myshlenie i Rech* translated by A. Sutton. Centre for Child Study, University of Birmingham.

VYGOTSKY, L.S. (1978). *Mind in Society.* Edited by M. Cole, V. John-Steiner, S. Scribner and E. Souberman. Cambridge, Mass.: Harvard University Press.

WANNER, E. and GLEITMAN, L.R. (Eds) (1982). *Language Acquisition: the State of the Art.* (Introduction) Cambridge: Cambridge University Press.

WEIR, R. (1962). *Language in the Crib.* The Hague: Mouton.

WELLS, C.G. (1974). Learning to code experience through language. *Journal of Child Language,* 1, 243–269.

WELLS, C.G. (1975a). The Contexts of Children's Early Language Experience. *Educational Review,* 27, 2, 114–125.

WELLS, C.G. (1975b). Interpersonal Communication and the Development of Language. Paper read at Third International Symposium on First Language Acquisition, London, September 1975.

WELLS, C.G. (1975c). *Coding Manual for the Description of Child Speech.* University of Bristol School of Education.

WELLS, C.G. (1976). 'Comprehension: What it means to understand', *English in Education,* 10, 2, 24–37.

WELLS, C.G. (1977). 'Language use and educational success: an empirical response to Joan Tough's *The Development of Meaning* (1977), *Research in Education,* 18, 9–34.

WELLS, C.G. (1978a). What makes for successful language development? In CAMPBELL, R. and SMITH, P. (Eds) *Advances in the Psychology of Language.* New York: Plenum Publ. Col.

WELLS, C.G. (1978b) *Language Development in Pre-School Children.* Final Report to the Social Science Research Council.

WELLS, C.G. (1979). Learning and using the auxiliary verb in English. In: LEE, V. (Ed) *Language Development.* London: Croom Helm.

WELLS, C.G. (1980). Adjustments in adult–child conversation: some effects of interaction. In: GILES, H., ROBINSON, W.P. and SMITH, P.M. (Eds) *Language: Social Psychological Perspectives.* Oxford: Pergamon

WELLS, C.G. (1981). *Learning through Interaction: the Study of Language Development.* Cambridge: Cambridge University Press.

WELLS, C.G. (1985a) *Language Development in the Pre-School Years.* Cambridge: Cambridge University Press.

WELLS, C.G. (1985b). Pre-school literacy-related activities and success in school. In: OLSON, D., TORRANCE, N. and HILDYARD, A. (Eds) *Literacy, Language and Learning.* Cambridge: Cambridge University Press.

WELLS, C.G. and FRENCH, P. (1980). *Language in the Transition from Home to School.* Final Report to the Nuffield Foundation.

WELLS, C.G., MACLURE, M. and MONTGOMERY, M.M. (1979). 'Some strategies for sustaining conversation'. In: *The Proceedings of the Sixth LACUS Forum* and in WERTH, P. (Ed) (1981) *Conversation, Speech and Discourse.* London: Croom Helm.

WELLS, C.G. and MONTGOMERY, M.M. (1981). 'Adult–child interaction at home and at school'. In: FRENCH, P. and MACLURE, M. (Eds) *Adult–Child Conversation.* London: Croom Helm.

WELLS, C.G. and NICHOLLS, J.C. (Eds) (1985) *Language and Learning: an Interactional Perspective.* Lewes, Sussex: Falmer Press.

WELLS, C.G. and RABAN, E.B. (1978). *Children Learning to Read.* Final Report to the Social Science Research Council.

WIGHT, J. (1975). 'Language through the looking glass', *Ideas,* 31, 13 London: University of London

WOOD, D. (1983). 'Teaching: natural and contrived', *Child Development Society Newsletter,* 31, 2–7.

WOOD, D. (in press). Talking to deaf children. University of Nottingham Department of Psychology. *Proceedings of the 8th National Conference of the Australian Association for Special Education.*